The
Sweet Life

Ida LeClair's
Guide to
Love & Marriage

Also from Islandport Press

Buy these and other great books at your local bookseller or
online at www.islandportpress.com.

Finding Your Inner Moose:
Ida LeClair's Guide to Livin' the Good Life
By Susan Poulin

John McDonald's Maine Trivia
By John McDonald, with illustrations by Mark Ricketts

Down the Road a Piece:
A Storyteller's Guide to Maine
By John McDonald

Bert and I . . . The Book
By Marshall Dodge and Robert Bryan

Headin' for the Rhubarb!
A New Hamsphire Dictionary (well, kinda)
By Rebecca Rule

Live Free and Eat Pie!
A Storyteller's Guide to New Hampshire
By Rebecca Rule

Not Too Awful Bad:
A Storyteller's Guide to Vermont
By Leon Thompson

The Sweet Life

Ida LeClair's
Guide to
Love & Marriage

by Susan Poulin

ISLANDPORT PRESS

Islandport Press, Inc.
P.O. Box 10
Yarmouth, Maine 04096
www.islandportpress.com
info@islandportpress.com

Text Copyright ©2016 by Susan Poulin
Illustrations Copyright © 2016 by Gordon Carlisle
First Islandport Press Edition published May 2016

ISBN: 978-1-939017-95-6
Library of Congress Card Number: 2015945271

Dean L. Lunt, publisher
Book jacket design by Teresa Lagrange
Book design by Michelle A. Lunt
Front & back cover images by Kevin Bennett

For Gordon
Thank you for taking this journey with me.

Table of Contents

Author's Note: Ida and Me

Ida came to me twenty years ago. I was thirty-eight and Ida was fifty, which seemed fairly old to me at the time. Now Ida is holding at sixty, and at fifty-eight, I'm catching up. When I reach sixty, my plan is for us to grow old together. And I'm looking forward to it!

In the four years since *Finding Your Inner Moose* was published, Ida and I have experienced many adventures together with more than two hundred performances, keynote speeches, book readings and author visits. We've criss-crossed the great state of Maine, traveled as far away as Maryland. We entertained women from twenty-two states and several Canadian provinces at the Delta Kappa Gamma Society International, 2013 Northeast Regional Conference in Portland, Maine. We created a new show, *I Married an Alien!,* and continue to write our weekly Maine humor blog, *Just Ask Ida* at JustAskIda.com.

Our newest adventure began in the autumn 2014 with the development of a television talk show. *The View From He'ah with Ida LeClair, Queen of North Country Chat* premiered in 2015 on PPMtv, streaming and on Ida's YouTube station, Ida TV. This half-hour format features a guest interview as well as an assortment of music, stories, advice and even boasts a poetry corner. Ida loves talking with folks (no surprise there!) and is a natural interviewer. This has lead to the development of *The View From He'ah Variety Show*, an expanded version of the television show. This show, hosted by Ida, features a rotating roster of fabulous guests and musicians, tours to theaters, and helps rasie money for non-profits.

And now a second book! You'd think that spending so much time with Ida would get old, but it doesn't. She continues to surprise and delight me. I'm fascinated at how her world unfolds to me and how things I'm experiencing flow through me and morph into Ida's life, transformed, but recognizable. And sure, Ida sometimes has more fun than I do and is definitely more resilient, but she's always there for me. A best friend and teacher, Ida gets me to look at things from a different point of view, she picks me up when I'm down and, boy, does she help me laugh at myself.

Truly, Ida is the gift that keeps on giving, and I am grateful to have her in my life.

Susan Poulin
May 2016

One

Puppy Love

Hello, my name is Ida LeClair. I live in Mahoosuc Mills, which is a small town in Western Maine. I married my high school sweetheart, Charlie, and we live in a beautiful double-wide mobile home with our little dog, Scamp. I work as a cashier down to the A&P.

I'm also a Certified Maine Life Guide, which is kind of like a Life Coach only without the diplomas, fancy schmancy office, personal stylist, and trainer. Life coaches tend to talk about self-care and processing your feelings and can be a little too woo-woo for me. Besides, I believe in living your life, not talkin' about it all the time. The way I see it, life guiding is more like a gentle nudge in the right direction. Someone to lend a hand when you need a little help getting out of the pucker brush and back onto the trail.

So if you're all jacked up to make a vision board, do affirmations, and visualize yourself to a happy marriage, you've come to the wrong place. But if you want some good old-fashioned, commonsensical advise, and are ready to get up off your duff

1

and do what needs to be done to make it happen, welcome aboard. I know there's a lot of books out there about relationships, and I'm tickled you chose mine.

So what qualifies me to write a book about marriage? Well, for one thing, forty-plus years of being married. It might not make me an "expert," but it certainly gives me *a lot* to talk about. And you know what? In a pinch, I'll take experience over book learnin' every time. Because there tends to be a gap between how things should be and how they really are, and trust me, if the gap's too big, you'll lose your way. But you can make that gap smaller, and that's what we're focusing on here.

In my first book, *Finding Your Inner Moose*, I talked about your relationship with yourself and how you can make your good life even better. This book is about sharing your better life with a mate. From time to time, I may borrow a story, advice, or anecdote from *Finding Your Inner Moose* to share here because it bears repeating. (Besides, if you're like me, sometimes you can't remember what you had for breakfast, so it'll feel just like new anyway).

Puppy Love

I can't remember a time in my life when I didn't know Charlie. See, Mahoosuc Mills is a small town, so he was always there in the background somewheres, plowing with his Dad, stackin' wood for Mrs. Thibodaux, riding his bike to Blue's general store to get some licorice or playing hockey or little league ball.

So, I've been trying to place exactly when Charlie moved from the back of the picture to the front. I think it happened kinda gradual. He was a couple years ahead of me in school. Close as I can place it, probably the last half of my freshman year was when I really took notice of Charlie in that special way. That's when my friend Dot started dating Tommy.

Charlie and Tommy were friends back then, still are. In fact, most of the folks we hung out with in high school, we hang out with now. Like I said, Mahoosuc Mills is a small town, the kind of place where roots run deep. So Dottie, me and the usual suspects—Celeste, Rita, Betty and Shirley—would be eatin' in the school cafeteria, and Tommy would come up to our table and start flirting with Dottie. Of course, there was much giggling and awkward pauses galore, but Tommy would hang in there and Dottie would sit there all flushed and moon-eyed. Usually, Charlie would be there with him, hanging back a bit, to be sure, but still taking everything in.

Then one day, I remember thinking, "Wow, Charlie sure has gotten tall. And when did he fill out like that?"

Gradually I realized he was no longer the boy I thought of when I thought of him. He was looking, well, like a man. But frankly, that seemed a little scary, him bein' a junior and all.

Still, skating parties on the pond behind Shirley's farm always seemed more fun if Charlie was there. He was a hot-shot on skates, and he liked skating in front of me, backwards. Before I knew it, he was my favorite hockey player. When he was on the ice, I cheered a little bit louder, and I might have been known to stand up and holler at the top of my lungs when he made a break toward the goal. In the cafeteria, I knew where Charlie was, and sometimes, I'd catch him lookin' at me.

Then came the Fourth of July party at Dottie's parent's camp. There was a whole gang of us there: Dottie's brother and his friends, Dot and Tommy's friends, and a few kids who just showed up. We had a cookout and spent the day hanging out on the dock, horsing around in the water, and swimming out to the float and diving off.

Charlie sat beside me during lunch. Can't remember what we talked about—I was too distracted by his bare arms resting on the table, our bathing suits almost touching, the heady aroma of burgers cookin' on the grill. I could barely think straight.

Then, right out of the blue, Charlie says, "Want to go out in a canoe?"

"What?" I replied. It kind of took me by surprise because, like I said, I was a little distracted.

"We can't swim for an hour. So what do you say we go for a paddle. You know, just something to do."

"Sure. Kind of boring just waiting," I say, pretending to be casual.

So off we went. I'll tell you, from the minute we got into that canoe, things just clicked. You know, some folks have a hard time paddling in sync. Some never can. But with Charlie and me, the paddlin' just flowed smooth and easy, one stroke after another.

And that was that. We stayed within sight of each other the rest of the day. After dark, there were firecrackers, sparklers, and the like, and we all sat around the campfire toastin' marsh-mallows, making s'mores and nursing our sunburns. I can still picture it, all our young faces visible in the glow of the firelight.

Later, Charlie asked me if I needed a ride home, and I said "yes" (which was certainly true, once I told Shirley I wasn't going to ride home in her car).

I can't recall much about that ride down the camp road to the highway, through Mahoosuc Mills and home, except for the smell of Coppertone and my thoughts racing. Will he kiss me? The feel of my hand in his, his thumb caressing my palm. (Remember what that was like, that electric feeling?)

And yes, he did kiss me. Just a little one, sweet and gentle. Oh baby, I still have a soft spot for Coppertone!

So began our summer of love. Between movies at the Strand, cookouts, and trips to the Dairy Joy, Charlie and me spent many a steamy evening up to the Moose Megantic Lake Overlook, otherwise know as Makeout Point.

A lot has change since then, but some things stay the same. Makeout Point? That's where the Sky Lodge Restaurant and Inn is now located. And holding hands has a different kind of pizzazz to it. It's more like slipping into your favorite pair of gloves. They may be a little worn, but they're still warm and, boy, are they comfortable.

> *And yes, he did kiss me. Just a little one, sweet and gentle. Oh baby, I still have a soft spot for Coppertone!*

And you know what? Every once and awhile, Charlie and me drive up to the Sky Lodge and park overlooking the lake. We never do go into the restaurant.

Makin' Whoopie!

A while back, I went on a whoopie pie kick. It started when I made some for the bake sale down to the Senior Center. Of course, I had to sample a couple, you know, for quality control. They were so good, I came home and made a batch for Charlie and me. God, there's nothing like a fresh-from-the-oven whoopie pie with a glass of cold milk!

In case you've never had one (and let me tell you, that is a sad state of affairs), a traditional whoopie pie is two cookie-sized rounds of chocolate cake with white frosting in between. Kind of like a sandwich, only way better! The frosting is usually made with vegetable shortening (that's how I like 'em), though some folks I know mix a little marshmallow fluff into theirs. And that's your basic whoopie pie. Easy peasy.

These days they come in lots of fancy schmancy flavors, what you might call your gourmet whoopie pies. You know, pumpkin with a cream cheese frosting, ginger bread filled with maple cream, lemon with raspberry butter cream, you name it. I even saw one place offering a *light* whoopie pie. To which I say, "Seriously? Why bother?" Oh, I've had some fancy whoopie pies and they were tasty, but I'm partial to the traditional chocolate one—I guess 'cause they bring back tasty memories.

> *I even saw one place offering a light whoopie pie. To which I say, Seriously? Why bother!*

A few years back, some folks pushed to name the whoopie pie as the official Maine Dessert, but, alas, the blueberry pie won that battle. People didn't give up, though, and in 2011, the whoopie pie was declared the official Maine State Treat. Of course, one sour puss made a big deal about honoring the whoopie pie, you know, claiming we were promoting obesity. I'm thinking, "Come on! It's called a *treat* for a reason." They're not lobbying to add the whoopie pie to the food pyramid! For cryin' in your chowdah! I'm sorry, but naming broccoli the official Maine State Treat, just wouldn't cut it in my book.

Amazingly, the whoopie pie is the focus of an even greater controversy—Maine, New Hampshire, and Pennsylvania all claim to be the birthplace of this delicacy. I'm goin' with Maine, of course, but in the end, who cares. The important thing is that some genius thought of it, God bless 'em!

Now as to the name, there are a few different stories about how it come to be called the whoopie pie. The Pennsylvania Amish say that whenever a farmer out in the field or some kid at school unwrapped his lunch and found one, they'd holler, "Whoopee!"

Our version is a little different. Back in the depression, this Maine woman was bakin' a cake and had some batter left over. She didn't want to waste it, so she put a couple of big spoonfuls onto a cookie sheet and baked it. Later, she slathered on some frosting, took a bite and exclaimed, "Whoopee, it worked!"

I like our story best because it rings true, doesn't it? There's a woman at the center, efficiently doing her job, facing down economic adversity, but improvising, being creative, trying something new, and being happily surprised by the outcome. It doesn't get much sweeter than that.

Besides, who but a woman would invent portable cake?

The Frostin' Holds it Together

So one night Charlie and me are enjoying freshly made whoopie pies, and he says, "You know, Ida, there may be fancier desserts, but an old fashioned whoopie pie doesn't disappoint."

"You got that right," I say. "They're sweet, simple, and easy."

"Kind of like a good marriage," and he gives my hand a squeeze.

It's sweet moments like that that make the rocky times worth it, right?

And that's how this whole book got going. Think about it: a whoopie pie is more than two halves coming together. You don't cook a blob of chocolate cake, cut it in half (which is hard to do without it falling apart) then smear some frosting on it, hoping it will all stick together. No, you cook two separate scoops of batter and when they're done (meaning they're cooked all the way through and won't fall apart when you pick 'em up), you put frosting on one piece. Sure, you could eat it like that—one round of cake with frosting—and it would be good. Seriously, you don't really need the other half. But if you do put it together with another chocolate cookie-like thing and add more frosting, it's *even* better.

A strong marriage is just like that—two wholes coming together, joined by love. That would be the frosting. It's what keeps things from breakin' apart, even if the edges get a little battered or one of the chocolate cakes cracks.

So that's what this book is about: how to keep your marriage sweet, simple, and easy. And when I say marriage, I don't care if you're husband and wife, boyfriend and girlfriend, husband and husband, wife and wife, or undecided (and good for you for keepin' your options open). In fact, many suggestions in this book also apply to your friendships and family relationships. In the end, it all comes down to how you treat yourself and how you treat others.

How to Use This Book

Just like with my first book, I knew I couldn't pull this off all by my lonesome. Marriage is not a one size fits all kind of thing. In each chapter, my husband Charlie will weigh in with a man's point of view. His sections are appropriately named, "Straight Talk From the Barcalounger." Throughout the book, I feature stories about my friends and other couples in Mahoosuc Mills. In "Love Mahoosuc Mills Style," I highlight some of those stories. And in each chapter, I've included "Recipes for Romance," which is exactly what it says.

Charlie and me were really looking forward to having children, but it just didn't work out. That said, I think my parents did a pretty good job of balancing kids and their relationship, so I'll be drawin' on the example they set as well as on other experts in the field, namely my sister, Irene, and my friends.

But, to be honest, I'm not gonna dwell on it because once you get past a certain age and your children are grown up (or what passes for it nowadays), it's basically just the two of you, and Charlie and me have lots of practice in that department.

I've noticed that self-help books tend to include action steps, but that just sounds too daunting. So, like in *Finding Your Inner Moose*, I'll close each chapter with a section I call "Gettin' Going." These are just little ideas to jazz up your relationship. They're not required, and not all of 'em will be of interest to you. Just cherry pick the ones that catch your eye. Marriage is like anything else in life: you get out of it what you put into it. If you want to make your good marriage even better, roll up your sleeves and get going!

> *If you want to make your good marriage even better, roll up your sleeves and get going!*

Word to the wise: If you find something in this book you'd like to try, you don't necessarily have to discuss it with your spouse. That might make it a bigger deal than necessary. First, try upping your game. It may gently nudge your mate into doing the same. If it works, you get to skip that whole "we need to talk about us" deal. If, after you've tried it for awhile and your spouse is still clueless, you may choose to work it into the conversation. If you decide to talk about it, make sure you're both in a good mood and having fun, not in the middle of an argument.

Let me assure you, you're not being sneaky. You're setting yourself up for success. I remember my Mom sayin' to me, "Marriage is not a 50-50, I'll meet him half way, kind of thing, Ida. It works best if you try to show up 150 percent, trusting your spouse will do the same. It's hard to do all the time, but if you're aiming for 150 percent, your average is gonna be a lot closer to 100 percent than if you're settling for 50 percent."

Straight Talk From the Barcalounger: Funny is Forever

I remember seeing Ida ridin' her bike when she was a kid, pigtails flying. I can't really say when that image changed, but it did. One day, in high school, I realized, "Geez, she's kinda cute." Still is. But that's not what hooked me.

You know how some gals are drop-dead gorgeous, but you find yourself thinking: Man, day in, day out, she'd be an assignment. What got my attention was Ida's smile and the way she looks at life. She's fun to be with, and God, she cracks me up! Plus, she's a good cook. I knew we could go the distance. Let's face it: beauty fades, but funny is forever.

Bridesmaids

As you may already know, back in Mahoosuc Mills, I hang out with a great group of gals—Celeste, Rita, Betty, Dot, Shirley, and me. We call ourselves The Women Who Run With the Moose. Yes, that's the same crew I sat with in the high school cafeteria all those years ago. We've been close since before Charlie and me started dating, so that makes our friendship my longest running non-family relationship. God what a group. No question, good friends are an essential part of marriage.

We've gone through good times and bad times together, and I've still got the bridesmaids dresses to prove it. And honey, no matter what they say, you cannot wear it again. There's just not that many occassions to wear a fuchsia ruffled concoction with a puffy full-length skirt, especially one that might look right at home in a Disney cartoon or, if it were crocheted, as a toilet-paper cover. Rita was responsible for that fuchsia disaster, and we still tease her about it. Yup, bridesmaids dresses prove the fact that one style does not flatter all body types, and some colors should never, ever be worn. Trust me.

I got around the color issue by dressing my bridesmaids in different shades of pastels. Let's see, Celeste wore peach. Rita, with her sunny disposition, wore yellow. Dot, wore seafoam green, and Betty was pretty in pink. Shirley sported the deepest shade of violet I could find because let's face it, some folks are not really pastel people. My sister, Irene, the maid of honor, had on the prettiest periwinkle blue. Matched her eyes.

Yup, bridesmaids dresses prove the fact that one style does not flatter all body types, and some colors should never, ever be worn. Trust me.

Back when Charlie and me got married, folks didn't do different style dresses on every bridesmaid. I was already pushin' the envelope with multiple colors. So, style-wise, I looked for something middle of the road. You know, not too hideous on someone. It was hard though, as Shirley tops out just shy of six feet, and Rita is shorter than me. I mean, short like old Catholic nun short. I'm 5'2" and I tower over her.

Betty hosted the bridal shower, so, of course, it was picture perfect. Afterall, Betty was givin' Martha Stewart a run for her money before Martha was *Martha*. All the decorations were pastel to match the bridesmaid's dresses. And everyone wore pastels to the event. (Not the guys because this was before th Jack and Jill shower thing.) There were even pastel-colored cupcakes and party favors, you name it.

The girls chipped in and bought me the most beautiful lacy negligee and robe in the lightest shade of pink—I mean, just a whisper of color. The ensemble left hardly anything to the imagination (though Charlie's always had a pretty good imagination!). I still remember the look on his face when I walked into the room wearing that lacy confection on our wedding night. Whoopie!

Our reception was held down to the Fish and Game, over on Duck Pond Road. One of my favorite wedding memories is of me and the girls spending the day before spiffin' up the place. Boy, did it ever need a good cleaning. But everyone rolled up their sleeves and pitched in. Then, we got down to business. Betty was in charge, of course, so the place was decorated to within an inch of its life, with crepe paper and balloons, streamers and all. We even gussied up the animal heads hanging on the walls.

> *And, we started a tradition that is only growing stronger in middle age—at least one of us got to laughing so hard, she peed her pants. No need to name names.*

They never did get the lipstick and mascara off a couple of them bucks. It was great fun! And, we started a tradition that is only growing more common in middle age—at least one of us got to laughing so hard, she peed her pants. No need to name names.

Recipes for Romance: Mom's Dessert

No matter who does most of the cooking—you, him, or your personal chef, Mr. Ronald McDonald—it's important to learn how to make a couple of things your husband's mother used to make for him (providing he liked her cooking). In the newlywed days, your cooking may be an adjustment for him. If he starts getting that deer in the headlight sort of look when he asks, "Ummm, what's for supper?" it's time to make one of these tried-and-true treats. They're comfortable and familiar, and will reassure him that he made the right decision marrying you. After his mother is gone, making one of her recipes will be even more special, something that makes him feel loved and cared for.

My mother-in-law, Simone, used to make Mom's Dessert, a refrigerator cake that is inexpensive and easy peasy. I don't know if she got it off a box of graham crackers or what. It sounds kind of weird, but give it a try and I think you'll be pleasantly surprised by how dense and tasty it is.

Basically, all you need are graham crackers, whipping cream, Hershey's Syrup, and sprinkles. First, you whip up the cream. Once it's whipped good, add Hershey's Syrup until it's nice and chocolaty. Break the graham crackers in half, so they're square. Take one and slather on the chocolate whipped cream. No need to be perfect with this, so it's a fun dessert to make with kids or grandkids. Put it on a plate, and do the same to another cracker. Place it on top of first one. Keep going until you get a little stack, then turn it on it's side to make a loaf. Keep layering the crackers and cream until it's as long as you want. Then you can add another row beside the first to make a square or wider rectangle. When it's as big as you want, frost the whole thing with more chocolate whipped cream. Cover it (use a Tupperware cake thingy or plastic wrap with toothpicks stuck into the cake to keep the wrap from touchin' the top). Put the dessert in the fridge, and let it set overnight. The next day, make it pretty by adding sprinkles. I use multicolored ones, and I've found if you put 'em on before the cake sets, they'll run. Dig in. Yumbo!

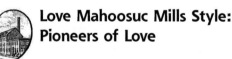 ## Love Mahoosuc Mills Style: Pioneers of Love

I remember a few years back, I'm sitting in the outhouse at my niece Caitlin's place, freezin' my you-know-what off, trying to relax enough to do my business and get outta there. As I watched my breath, I'm thinking, "Ida, you are *not* a pioneer." And honestly, I never wanted to be a pioneer. And I thank God every day I was born when I was, so I don't have to be a pioneer.

Caitlin and her boyfriend Adam invited Charlie and me and her parents (my sister Irene and her husband Jimbo) over for brunch. The kids were livin' in a winter rental up to Moose Megantic Lake, this tiny cabin heated only by a wood stove. Beautiful location, don't get me wrong, but it was a tad rustic for my taste. Three miles in on a dirt road. I don't think so!

Caitlin works down to Mahoosuc Health Food and does a little Feng Shui consulting on the side. She even teaches a class in Feng Shui down to Adult Ed. Plus, she's part of what she calls an "art collective." I honestly don't know what that is, exactly. They do have a storefront downtown with a little gallery. Right now, Caitlin's doing these little paintings of broken pottery. Jury's still out (and frankly, I never thought I'd say this), but I'm kind of missing that art she did featuring them marshmallow Peeps.

I can hear Adam whistling away as he's haulin' in wood for the stove, happy as a clam. Adam picks up hours at Mahoosuc Health Food, too, and also works part-time in a music store down to Bangor. Plus, he's always in one band or another. The one he's in now is called Who Goosed the Moose (or something like that). He plays bass and Caitlin says he's pretty good on the kazoo, too (although I am not really sure how you judge that). The two of them met at our yard sale a few years back. Caitlin was helping me out, and Adam stopped by to check out the record albums or "vinyl," as he calls them. Tickles me to think about it, the two of 'em with matching nose rings, flirting up a storm.

Anyways, we're all crammed into this little cabin, eating vegetable frittata (delicious), zucchini bread (let me say, if you're not used to whole-wheat flour, it can kind of overwhelm) and exotic fruit salad with mangos and kiwis and, well, a couple of things I have never seen down to the A&P. The coffee was out of this world, of course, because if kids these days know one thing, it's coffee. It was strong. Caitlin was serving it with some kind of frothed-up milk. After half a cup, all of us were talking a mile a minute!

I says to Caitlin, "I'm probably not gonna sleep until Tuesday, but darn, this coffee's good!"

The payback for all that good java, or course, was this trip to the outhouse. Just when I was getting comfortable; on with the coat, the boots, the hat, the gloves . . .

Anyhoo, mission accomplished, I carefully make my way back to the cabin, hoping I don't fall and break a hip. I come inside in time to see Adam presenting Caitlin with a little sprig from a fir tree. "For my sweetie," he says, and Caitlin's face lights up like it's a bouquet of roses. They exchange a little kiss, and Adam's hand lingers on the small of her back as she turns to froth more milk.

On the way home I says to Charlie, "Remember when we were first married, living in that tiny apartment over Mrs. Nadeau's?"

"Sure, how could I forget? Waking up to them loggin' trucks rumbling by."

"Well, we were just starting out. We fixed it up cute, though, with all that second hand stuff. Felt like we were playing house."

"That or playing doctor." With that, Charlie takes my hand in his, raises it to his lips, and gives it a gentle kiss.

We smile, and hold hands all the way home to our cozy doublewide with the furnace humming, an inside bathroom down the hall, and our little dog, Scamp, crazy to see us as we pull in the drive.

There's something to be said for being married a good long time, but every now and then it's nice to look back and remember how it was when we first got together. Like most couples, Charlie and me have been through good times and not so good times, but, wow, what a journey. And you know what? I'd do it all again in a heart beat.

Gettin' Going

- Talk about when you first met. Bring it up kind of spontaneous, maybe over dinner, and see what happens.
- Do something you used to do when you first started dating, you know, when you were making an effort. Put on some lipsick or maybe his favorite perfume.
- Partners and/or husbands: bring her flowers just because.
- If his mother is still alive, learn how to make one of his favorites from the master. If you already have one of her recipes, make it for no special reason, just to do something nice.
- Make a night of it. Combine two or all three of the above.

Two

Getting Back to Basics

Relationships are not rocket science, though sometimes it feels like sending a rocket into space would be easier. People have been coupling up since the dawn of time. That's before cell phones and computer dating, before couples counseling and prenuptial agreements, before manscaping and the Brazilian (which I learned about recently and, let me tell you, I'm still in shock).

As with anything else that you want to last, it's best to lay a good foundation before adding on the fancy schmancy stuff. Then if things start feelin' a little wonky, you know what to do—get back to basics.

That said, if you kind of skimped on the foundation, and now find yourself with only a little crawl space, you can still choose to build a better foundation. It starts with showing up, getting your priorities straight, respecting each other, and taking care of yourself.

Number-One Priority

I learned about marriage from my parents. They were married just shy of fifty years, and they had the kind of good, strong marriage that only time and commitment deliver. As Dad says, "A good marriage is like a good fire; you have to tend it to make it burn bright."

Growing up, our parents used to tell Irene and me, "Our number-one priority is to each other, you girls second. Because if we don't take care of our marriage, it won't be strong enough to support this family."

That may sound shocking nowadays when people focus on putting children first. But as a kid, I found this notion comforting. First off, our parents told us outright what they were doing. Kids love to know what's going on. Second, our parents never felt guilty about spending time together without us girls. They didn't believe they were doing anything wrong, so Irene and me didn't either. And third, they were always so happy when they got back from a breakfast out or an overnight in Bangor. Of course, we still did a lot of stuff as a family. Except for their dates, they took us most everywhere with them. Spending time with Irene and me never seemed like an obligation to our parents. They were energized in their relationship, and they shared that energy and enthusiasm for life with us.

Looking back, I realize that my parents didn't have a lot of extra money, but they always managed to scrape together enough for a date. Sometimes they just bought a couple of beers at Blue's General Store, drove up to the Moose Megantic Lake Overlook, parked, and talked (or whatever). It wasn't about spending money, it was about spending time together—just the two of them.

Making a good marriage even better doesn't have to be a big, complicated thing—just showing up is a good beginning. But trust me, that's harder than it sounds because it's easy to get caught up in the issues of life and before you know it, you're MIA from your relationship.

> *Making a good marriage even better doesn't have to be a big, complicated thing—just showing up is a good beginning.*

Down Home Holiday Festival

The second weekend in December, Mahoosuc Mills holds its annual Down Home Holiday Festival. It used to be the Down Home Christmas Festival, but we are now politically correct. The Saint Hyacinth Christmas Bazaar is part of the Festival. I suppose we should call it the Holiday Bazaar, but hey, we're Catholic! Who are we kiddin'?

Oh, the town's decorated real cute, and all the stores are open. You got your Kiwanis Club selling trees in the vacant lot where Pomaleau's store used to be, a horse drawn sleigh for the kids up to Bucky Dumont's field, and out on Enchanted Mountain, really a little bunny slope with a rope tow, the Rotary Club makes an ice slide and runs a toboggan race (helmets and costumes required). Oh God, folks really get into that toboggan race, and you should see some of their outfits. I think my favorite was when the Lambert brothers dressed up like the Beatles and tricked out their toboggan to look like a yellow submarine. Half way down they hit a bump, and their wigs went flying. God, did we laugh!

The Women Who Run With the Moose have a table down to Saint Hyacinths where we sell crafts. It's the second most popular booth at the Christmas Bazaar (well, third really, if you count the baked goods table). The most popular, hands down, is

the Blessed Bling Boutique. I swear, the deals in that booth are
unreal!

Every year us girls pick a theme for our craft table, and this
last one, it was "Drink Safe." We considered it a community service. You know, there are so many parties during the holidays.
Plus, it's cold and flu season. There's nothing more disconcerting
than being at a party and accidentally drinking out of someone
else's bottle, can, or glass because they all look the same. You ever
done that? Yuck-a-rooney! So, we were gearing up to sell crocheted beer cozies in a wide variety of colors and designs. (Mine
had snowflakes on 'em.) Talk about practical, not only do they
make it easy to recognize your beer can, but they keep the beer
cold and your hands warm. They don't call it a cozy for nothing!

We were also makin' these cute wine glass markers. You
know, those little things you put on your wine stem so you
know which glass is yours? Betty found the idea on the Pinter-
est. We got everything we needed down to The Beaded Moose
(How perfect is that?) in Bangor. Heck, we had so much fun
there, we're gonna take some sort of beading class together,
when we get around to it. So anyways, you make the wine
glass markers with your basic hoop earrings and some pretty
beads. We had a blast putting them together, and, gosh, they
were adorable, if I do say so myself.

What with crocheting those beer cozies and getting together
with the gals to put together the wine glass markers, I was pretty
busy, especially in the two weeks leading up to the Festival.
Throw in my book club potluck and cookie swap, Christmas
shopping, and extra hours down to the A&P (one of our main
cashiers, Shannon Fournier, slipped on the ice and broke her
wrist), and I was busier than a one-armed paper hanger. Why, I
don't think Charlie and me ate dinner together once.

Then, one morning toward the end of the week, I was eating breakfast, off in my own little world, when I realize Charlie's staring at me.

"Did you say something, dear?" I ask.

"I've been talking to you for the last five minutes, but you haven't heard a darn thing I'm saying."

"I'm sorry, Charlie. I guess I'm a little distracted thinking about all I have to do. What were you saying?"

"Forget it. Not important."

And he stands up and gets ready to leave for work.

"The Festival is this weekend, and then things will get back to normal. Promise."

"I sure hope so. See you tonight."

"Oh, Charlie?"

"Yup?"

"I won't be home for dinner, but there's leftover baked ziti is in the fridge. Just heat it up with the extra sauce in the jar and melt some cheese on top."

Charlie grunted, grabbed his lunch, and out the door he went.

Yikes! That's a penalty flag if I ever saw one. Time to cook Charlie one of his favorite meals and get back on the up and up, because even the best marriage in the world can get a little off course if you're missing in action.

Showin' Up

It's common sense. A relationship works best if you actually spend some time physically and mentally in the same room. You know, paying attention to your mate, and really seeing them.

Now, I'm not saying you should shut off your television and stare adoringly into each other's eyes every evening. That's just not practical, and anyway, you'd get behind on your shows. But how about when you're eating a meal together? Try asking questions and really listening to your mate.

Or say he likes watching a game on the weekend. You couldn't care less. I get that. But is there a project you can do while sitting in the same room—maybe knitting or reading a magazine or doing your nails? You don't have to do it every game (that would be overkill), but if you've been real busy and you haven't seen him much, it can get things on an even keel. I have a craft room, right? But after that morning leading up to the Down Home Holiday Festival I just told you about, I decided to set up a card table in the den and make that my craft and gift wrapping headquarters until I was out of the woods.

Think about it: unless you're retired, you don't really spend that much time with your spouse—breakfast, maybe, and dinner, evenings, and some time on the weekends. So, make the most of it. Really show up and be with the person you decided to share your life with. It's kinda nice.

Recipe for Romance: Meat Loaf and Apple Pie

One of Charlie's favorite meals is your basic meat loaf, mashed potatoes, corn, and apple pie. Most of the time, I make the meat loaf with ground turkey because it's better for you. Or you can do half turkey and half hamburger. But sometimes extraordinary measures are called for, and only 100 percent ground beef will do. I know from past experience not to put any fancy twists into this meal. Charlie doesn't go in for that and this dinner is about him, not me.

To make the meat loaf, you throw your beef, an egg, green pepper, onion, a piece of bread, salt, pepper, and a few dashes of Worcestershire Sauce into a big bowl. You could add in some mushrooms and celery. Mix it up good. Works best to get in there with your hands and moosh it around. (Take your rings off before doing this or they'll get all yucky.) Put the meat mixture into a loaf pan. I grease it a little with some olive oil before I do. Top with ketchup and some grated cheese. I use the fancy, pre-shredded asiago or parmesan that you can buy at the A&P, because Charlie's worth it. Bake at 350 degrees for an hour or so.

I put plenty of butter in the mashed potatoes and a little canned milk (Simone, Charlie's Mom did that, and that's what he likes). Unless corn is in season, I use frozen corn, again with butter.

I prefer McIntosh apples for cooking (Pink Ladies, for eating). Usually, I make my own pie crust. It's a family recipe that I'm not at liberty to share. But if crusts get you down, buy pre-made ones at the supermarket. I just peel the apples and then cut them right into the pie plate on top of the bottom crust, sprinkle with a little white sugar and a little brown sugar (don't make it too sweet because the ice cream you're going to serve with it will do the heavy lifting). Add in some cinnamon, a little nutmeg, and a dash or two of ground cloves. Dot with butter, and put on the top crust. Don't forget to put a few cuts in the top for venting. Then, I pour a little milk into my hands and smear that on to the top of the crust. Use a paper towel to mop up the excess. Cook at 400 degrees for about a half hour, maybe a little more.

Serve with love!

The Power of Please and Thank You

So the other day, I'm on the phone to this catalogue company, when they launch into the usual spiel: "You're a valuable customer, blah, blah, blah, blah, blah . . . The next available representative will be with you in a moment."

And I say, "Thank you!" It's a recording for God's sake!

I continue listening to a touching rendition of "Yesterday" for a minute or two, when I hear, "Your call is important to us. Thank you for waiting."

"You're welcome!" I reply. Seriously.

It's a reflex, like blinking or breathing. See, good manners were drilled into me by my parents. There's no getting around it. Not that I'd want to. Being polite is a good thing, and has served me well over the years.

It was hard getting the hang of it at first, though. In our house, you had to say "please," "thank you," and "you're welcome." End of story. There was none of this, "Now what do you say?" kind of thing. My parents had their own method for showing my sister Irene and me how it's done.

"Pass the potatoes," I'd say at the dinner table, and my parents would act like they didn't hear me.

"Pass the potatoes," I'd repeat, a little louder. Still no response.

"Dad, pass the potatoes!"

Silence.

Then the penny drops.

"Please?"

"Here you go, Sweetie," Dad says, passing the potatoes.

"Thank you!" You had to follow up with that, or the potatoes disappeared to the other side of the table again.

"You're welcome."

Charlie was raised the same way. Oh, he was always polite, holding the door open for me, like a gentleman. Still does.

To this day, we say please and thank you to each other, not just for the big things, but for the smallest things, too. "Thanks for mowing the lawn, Charlie."

"Ida, please pass me that delightful little Mrs. Claus salt shaker you got down to the Christmas Tree Shop."

> *"Ida, please pass me that cute little Mrs. Claus salt shaker you got down to the Christmas Tree Shop." (Well, I embellished that one a little, but you get the idea.)*

(Well, I embellished that one a little, but you get the idea.)

Saying please and thank you is a sign of respect, which, in my opinion, is one of the most important things in a relationship. It lets your mate know you see all he or she is doing and appreciate it. Try adding please, thank you, and appreciation to your next to-do list, and see what happens.

Guest Towels and Other Mysteries

Putting things back where you found 'em is a sign of respect, and not doing so is a pet peeve of mine. After forty years of marriage, progress has been made on some things. Charlie now puts the toilet seat down, no problem. He finally signed on to replacing the toilet-paper roll when he uses the last of it (even if he does put it on backwards). But there is still room for improvement—especially replacing hand towels.

Like last fall, I'm having Celeste, Rita, Betty, Dot, and Shirley over to celebrate Celeste's birthday, right? Got the place all spiffed up, per usual. I wish I could be more relaxed when entertaining, but I just can't. It's important to me that everything's looking good, clean and tidy. I set the table the day before, so's not to get jammed up last minute and I splurged on some fresh flowers.

Everything's looking pretty darn near perfect when I leave for the A&P that morning. See, I get out of work at five, and the girls were coming over around six, so I wanted to hit the ground running.

I had an uneventful day at work, and I'm feeling upbeat when I get home. Until I walk into the house. Oh, my God! All over the floor: dirt and grass!

There's this trail of crud from the back door to the bathroom, where the towels are a wreck—all grimy and scattered about all willy-nilly. In the kitchen, dirty dishes are scattered over the counter and the cabinet doors are all ajar. It seemed like every other drawer was open a crack. Was the house ransacked by robbers? Nope. Just my husband!

See, Charlie worked Labor Day, so he was owed a day off. As luck would have it, this was the day, and he devoted it to clearing away some of the blow down from the latest tropical storm. Cripes! By the looks of things, he might as well have dragged half the debris into the double-wide to work on while watching the game!

Now, him leaving every drawer open and every cabinet door ajar is not a new thing I'm afraid. Charlie never seems to close anything all the way. He's always leaving his side of the sliding closet door open, so I close it, right? And then he goes, "I'm not done in there!" Likewise, his bureau drawers are always ajar. I just don't get it! It takes as much effort to not quite close a drawer as it does to close it all the way.

So, I'm standing there aghast, Dustbuster in hand, when Charlie pokes his head in the door.

"You're home early," he says by way of greeting.

"Just after five, same as usual," I say kinda frosty. Okay, a lot frosty.

"Huh, musta lost track of time."

"That's not all you lost track of, Buster."

"What?"

"Look at this place!"

"What?"

"Charlie! The girls are coming over."

"Yeah," he says, coming inside, giving me a quick kiss hello, "I better get in the shower, so I'm outta your hair before they get here. Meeting Bud, Smitty, Pat, Tommy, and Junior (the Husbands of the Women Who Run With the Moose) down to the Brew Ha Ha."

"Look at this mess! The Dustbuster won't even make a dent. Why didn't you take your work boots off when you came in?"

"Hey, I had a lot to do today, Ida. I couldn't put my boots on and off every time I wanted to take a leak, or get a snack or something."

> *God bless him, the guy's clueless. I mean, he's not being a wiseacre. He genuinely does not know which towels are the guest towels and which towels are the regular house towels.*

"And how many times have I told you the guest towels in the bathroom are for the guests?"

"What am I supposed to use?"

"Our regular towels!"

He just gives me a blank look. "Which ones are those exactly?"

God bless him, the guy's clueless. I mean, he's not being a wiseacre. He genuinely does not know which towels are the guest towels and which towels are the regular house towels.

27

That's when I take a deep breath and think, take a chill pill, Ida, and get over yourself. Charlie spent his day off working in the yard. You know he shows his love by doing, not talking, and so he just spent the whole day loving you up. Are you going to toss that out the window for a couple of guest towels?

"Thanks for all your work in the yard today, Charlie. It looks great."

"Needed to be done," he says, smiling. "I best take that shower and get myself gone."

And off he goes, a little bounce in his step.

I toss aside the overwhelmed Dustbuster, whip out my Kenmore, and make short work of the crud on the floor. Power vacuuming also helped me work off any leftover irritation. Trust me, it took me less time to set the house to rights than to stand in the bathroom doing another show and tell with towels like I'm Martha Stewart.

Shut It, Bub!

Still, I only wish there were a special alarm system to help fix the open drawer, cabinet, and closet problem. If there were, honey, I'd order a whole case. I dream about the commercial:

Does your spouse constantly leave drawers open, perhaps with a sock or two sticking out? Are closet doors left ajar, giving company a lovely view of a pile of shoes? In the kitchen, does it look like a bomb just hit, leaving all cabinets and drawers akimbo?

Well, your worries are over with the amazing "Shut It, Bub!"

This state-of-the-art alarm system will sound automatically when your spouse walks away from a closet, drawer, or cabinet without shutting it. Using special laser-sensory motion detectors developed for the Louvre, and only recently made available for domestic use, "Shut It, Bub!" can accomplish in just a few short weeks what you've been unable to do in years of marriage! Choose from a variety of alarm options: the New England fog horn, elementary school fire alarm, or police siren. Or, buy the deluxe "Shut It, Bub!" equipped with a digital voice reproduction system, offering personalized alarms like General George Patton ordering your husband to "Shut it, Bub!"

We even offer an alarm with Elvis Presley singing: "Shut it, bub, shut it, bub. Take that door and shut it, bub, uh huh huh."

Or your spouse's mother shouting out: "Were you raised in a barn?"

To order call 1-800-Shut-Bub. That's 1-800-Shut-Bub. Order today and we'll include, absolutely free, a toilet seat bonus. If your toilet seat is left up by your spouse, he will hear Clint Eastwood as "Dirty Harry", saying "You gotta ask yourself one question: do I feel lucky? Well do ya, punk? Now drop that seat and flush!"

Put the lid on these perennial problems once and for all with the amazing "Shut It, Bub!"

It's cheaper than a divorce!

A gal can dream, can't she?

 ## Straight Talk From the Barcalounger: A Happy Wife Makes for a Happy Husband

As I said in *Finding Your Inner Moose*, one simple key to a happy marriage is: Look interested and say, "Yes, dear."

You think I'm joking, but it's true! And tell her she looks nice. Took me a while to catch on to that last one. Sure, if we were going out on the town and she was all dolled up, I'd say something. But that's not enough—tell her everyday.

Whether the two of you are going to a bean supper, or she's off for a girls' night out, or if she's just going to work, your wife's put some effort into how she looks. Even if you feel she's missed the mark, compliment her. Say something like, "Don't you look sharp tonight, dear?" or "Aren't you something?" You're not being dishonest. You're showing her you notice and appreciate her. It's about rewarding effort. Trust me, just doing this one thing will improve the quality of your married life to no end, because a happy wife makes for a happy husband.

Love Mahoosuc Mills Style: Know Who's In Charge

I was out walkin' Scamp awhile back and ran into Pearl Plaisted dead-heading geraniums in her yard.

"Ida!" she says, "I haven't seen you all summer. Why don't you come in for some iced tea, dear?"

"Sounds good!" I reply. "It's some hot out, huh?"

Pearl, who is getting along in years, tried to stand but seemed to get stuck in the "half way up" position. I helped her the rest of the way up and into the house we go.

"Hank," she yells, "you decent? Ida's here."

Our dog, Scamp, loves goin' over to Hank and Pearl's place because that means he gets to terrorize their cat Tiki, named after Tiki Barber, the football player.

Sitting on the screened in porch, we got to talkin' about the big celebration coming up down to the Knights of Columbus. Get this: Frank and Ada Jones are going to celebrate their seventy-seventh wedding anniversary. Just you imagine! Frank is deaf as a post. Says he got that way out of self-defense because Ada could talk the ears off a dead donkey.

"Well," Ada's been known to look straight at him and retort, "now I know why my eyesight's shot!"

"Seventy-seven years," Hank says, shaking his head. "People have gotten purple hearts for less."

Pearl just rolls her eyes, offering me a homemade ginger snap.

"Of course, Pearl and me been happily married for thirty-five years," Hank continues.

Pearl chimes in, "More like twenty-five, I figure."

See, this is a well-honed routine.

"Wait a minute," I says, "I know for a fact that the two of you have been married over fifty years. You must be doin' something right. All joking aside . . . "

> *Frank is deaf as a post. Says he got that way out of self-defense 'cause Ada could talk the ears off a dead donkey.*

"Oh, we wouldn't want to do that," Hank says.

"Do what?" I ask.

"Put all joking aside, because you gotta have a sense of humor, or you're just not gonna make it as a couple."

"Ain't that the truth," Pearl adds. "If we weren't able to laugh at ourselves, I doubt we'd have survived the first ten years."

"Yup, those are the hardest."

"So many changes, and just as you're gettin' used to each other, a baby or two comes along."

"Money's tight, and you're trying to make ends meet."

"Make it through those first ten, then things sort of settle down and you kinda hit your stride."

"Yes, sir-ee. By the time you hit the ten-year mark, she knows who's boss. The key is having one person in charge," Hank says, pointing to himself and grinning. "You know, one person calling the shots. Right, Pearl?"

"That's right, dear. Oh, look, there's the mail truck. I'm expecting some photos of little Emma. She's our brandy new

> *"The number one key to a happy marriage, Ida, is to never let him know that the person who's really in charge is you."*

great-granddaughter, Ida. Cute as a button. Hank, you mind getting the mail, dear?"

"Will do. Time I got back to work, anyways."

"And don't forget, we're having supper with Phil and Ester tonight."

"Darn! What time we leavin'?"

"About five, five-fifteen. So you need to stop work by four-thirty, Hank, latest."

"Cuts my day short."

"I know, but I'm makin' lemon meringue pie for dessert. Is that motivation enough for you?"

"Okay, Okay. 4:30."

And off he goes to get the mail and attend to whatever pressing business is waiting for him in the shed.

Pearl waits until he clears the front of the house, turns to me and smiles. "The number one key to a happy marriage, Ida, is to never let him know that the person really in charge is you."

Sleep As a Marital Aid

Last winter, I got a wicked cold. Remember when you were young and a cold lasted about three days; five days tops? Now a cold drags on for days, maybe a week before you can see any discernable improvement. Then it just lingers for another week or two and you can't stop coughing. Even worse, it's not unusual to feel better for a bit, then get sucker punched with a relapse.

Anyhoo, I had me one of them corkers, and my butt was dragging. I hadn't gotten to the coughing stage yet. I was stuck at the "my head's too big to fit through the door" phase.

32

So on day three, it's nine in the evening, and I'm on my way to bed when Charlie says, "I'm gonna sleep in the Barcalounger tonight, dear."

"You don't have to do that, Charlie."

"You need your shut eye in order to get better, Ida. "

"Thanks, Charlie. I know I've been pretty restless what with this stuffy nose."

"You've been rockin' and rollin' that's for sure," Charlie said. "I'll be fine in the Barcalounger."

"You're a sweetheart," I said, and I actually got a little teary because I didn't feel good. "No need for both of us to get sick. Time for bed, Scamp."

That was so thoughtful of Charlie. Or maybe it's just self preservation, because you can't underestimate the power of sleep as a marital aid. All your best intentions can go out the window if you don't get enough sleep.

I like getting seven to eight hours of sleep a night. I feel pretty good when that happens. Of course, I don't do that without the usual interruptions. No, I generally wake up two to three times a night, sometimes every couple of hours. (Yes, I look at the clock.) But boy, if I get three or four hours uninterrupted sleep, that is a wonderful thing!

Charlie, on the other hand, sleeps through it all. How can I tell? The snoring, of course. Let's just say, he keeps a running commentary going all night long.

If I get less than seven hours of sleep, we're getting into the danger zone. Less than six hours and I probably shouldn't leave the house. Heck, I probably shouldn't even be left alone in the house.

Because I'm writing this book, I decided to do a little internet research on sleep deprivation. I wander over to WebMD, like you do (which, FYI, is not for the faint of heart, let me tell you), and find a sobering little number called, "Ten Surprising Effects of Lack of Sleep." I'll give you the highlights:

First off, being sleep deprived impairs your judgment, your memory and causes accidents. (No surprises there.) What was surprising was that it can cause not only car accidents, but disasters like Three Mile Island and Chernobyl. Yikes! Who knew? It's all pretty depressing which is funny because depression is also a side effect of sleep loss, along with aging your skin, weight gain, forgetfulness, and reduced sex drive. Sounds an awful lot like menopause, doesn't it? Which is another thing that effects your sleep. And we're back to where we started!

Needless to say, it's hard to show up in your relationship if you're not getting enough sleep. Then there's the cranky factor. Please, thank you and appreciation are quickly replaced with overwhelmed, whining, and resentment. Not very attractive!

> We have a queen-size at home, but with a king, it's like you're sleeping in separate zip codes!

When in doubt, sleep it out! Charlie and my vacations became more fun when we started paying attention to sleep. Meaning, if we're in a hotel, we get a king-sized bed. We have a queen-size at home, but with a king, it's like you're sleeping in separate zip codes! If we can't get a king, we take two double beds and sleep separate because it takes awhile to adjust to a new bed, and we don't want to keep the other one up.

Doesn't sound romantic, but it is. Bottom line: a well-rested spouse is more fun. You laugh together and have an easier time making decisions. Things just click, you're all simpatico, and before you know it, you're sneaking into each other's bed for a little together time. Then, back to your bed for a good night's sleep. Now that's what I call a romantic getaway!

Anyway, back to that bad cold I had. After a few good night's sleep, things started to turn around for me, and slowly I got better. Soon, Charlie was back in the big bed, as we call it. It really made me appreciate how warm and comforting it is having Charlie snoring beside me.

I gotta tell you though, even when Charlie was sleeping in the Barcalounger, he still came into the bedroom and we made the bed together every morning. This is something my parents did, and Charlie and me have carried on the tradition. It's such a simple thing to do, but it has real impact. Think about it. You're starting the day off as a team, doing a task together, putting things in order so they're nice to come home to. You can't get more basic than that.

Gettin' Going

- Ban all electronics during meal time. Folks my age can get all worked up about kids looking at their cell phones at the dinner table, yet think nothing of having the television on. In fact, go one step further and get rid of other distractions, too, like the newspaper, the latest romance novel you're reading, and the computer. Too overwhelming? Start with one meal a week and work up to one meal a day.
- Been overcommitted lately? Invest some time in your relationship. It doesn't have to be a big deal, just go for a walk or take in a movie. Cook your mate his favorite dinner and focus on him during the meal. Ask questions and really listen to the answers.

- Say please and thank you to your spouse. Don't make a big deal out of it—just do it.
- We all have our pet peeves. When you're both in a good mood (can't stress this enough) ask your spouse what theirs is. This is not a get everything off your chest, itchin' for a fight type deal. Come up with one pet peeve each (mine would be closing drawers, closets, and cabinets), and both of you try to eliminate that behavior for a week. Chances are, the change will stick for longer than that.
- If you're like me, the older you get, the longer it takes to get ready to do anything; going to bed is no exception. We plan time for the kids to get ready for bed, and it works for adults, too. Set a getting-ready-for-bed time, so you can get the sleep you need to show up in your relationship rested and ready to go.
- Start the day off right. Make the bed together. If you get up at different times during the week, try it on the weekend.

Three

There is no "I" in Team, but Maybe There Should Be

You know that scene in *Jerry Maguire* where Tom Cruise (looking cute as ever) says, "You complete me?" He starts to go on, but Renee Zellweger whimpers, "You had me at Hello."

Remember that?

What a load of hooey.

I just don't go in for this "you complete me" crap. It's creepy! Remember our whoopie pie from chapter one? A good relationship is two wholes coming together, joined by love. No completing necessary. If you both show up with your whole self, one person isn't left alone to do all the heavy lifting.

Here's my rewrite for Renee, and she can still get teary if she wants to. Breakin' up is hard to do, but, honey, this guy is too little, too late. How about she says, "You should have stopped at hello." She gives him a little hug, "Blah, blah, blah . . . had some good times together . . . blah blah . . . we can still be friends," and shows him the door. Then her girlfriends, who are already there (very handy), tell her she made the right decision. They cry, eat, drink, laugh, talk about old boyfriends and a couple years down the road, Renee's saying things like, "Boy, did I ever make the right decision with that guy!"

The "Not a Crappy Day" Option

Being happy is a choice.

It comes from the inside, not the outside. Once you realize that, you can let go of the notion that someone else can make you happy. And, (wahoo!), you can stop working so hard to make other people happy. Sure, you can still do nice things for them, as long as you know that whether they're happy or not is up to them.

When you're feeling low, generally husbands will try to solve the problem. That's how they're wired, which can be a good thing or irritating as all get out if you just want to wallow a bit (wallowing being the important first step in the choosing to be happy process). Wives, on the other hand, try to make him feel better. Hard going because he probably just wants some space and doesn't need you there, talking him to death, encouraging him to turn that frown upside down. He's the one that needs to do that. Put your energy elsewhere, like baking him some cookies.

Of course choosing to be happy doesn't mean that nothing bad ever happens. Oh, contraire! Life is full of FGOs or Friggin' Growth Opportunities as my cousin Mikey calls them. It's what you do with those opportunities that counts.

For example, one Saturday morning last summer, I was out running errands, when I noticed that the air conditioning in my car wasn't pulling its weight. Interesting. Still, I continued on my way, now and then putting my hand over the vent, to see if it was my imagination. It wasn't.

Then, I'm turning onto Mill Road, when my car starts beeping at me. What the hell? I'm looking at my dash, but can't see anything lit up. Now, I'm really starting to get hot under the collar (and I have no AC). I pull over in a shady spot and, with the glare gone, I can see that the temperature light is on. I look at the gauge, and it's almost on "H," so I put the heat on high and open the windows (an old trick my Dad taught me). As the arrow on the temperature gauge slowly drifts down, so does my mood.

As I'm sitting there, I remembered an incident that happened a couple of weeks back as I was heading off to my book club. See, we usually take the summer off, and this was to be our last get together until September. Instead of meeting at night, we were having a Saturday cookout-type thing. You know, review our year, vote for our favorite book, worst ending, best love scene, etc. I didn't want to rush around too much in the morning, so being all organized like I am, I'd made this nice potato salad the night before.

So by mid-day Saturday, I'm all dressed and ready to go. I grab the bowl from the fridge, but as I turn the bowl hits the fridge door, slips outta my hand, and down it goes, smash! The green ceramic bowl from my grandmother's set, one of my all-time favorites, shatters into a million pieces. And my beautiful potato salad is kaput. Scamp, alerted by my questionable language, runs in to investigate.

"No!" Charlie goes, "Scamp, get back!"

Scamp retreats to supervise from under the kitchen table, and Charlie, bless his heart, calmly helps me deal with the mess.

"Don't worry, Hon. We'll find you another one of these bowls at a yard sale or something."

Meanwhile, the clock's ticking. Now I need to improvise, pick something up on the way. There's no getting around it, I'm going to be late, which doesn't sit well with me.

"Why don't you just go?" suggests Charlie. "I'll deal with the rest of it."

"No, no."

> *I ladle my not-so-beautiful potato salad into another bowl, all the while thinking, "Well, isn't this is going to be a crappy day!"*

I ladle my not-so-beautiful potato salad into another bowl, all the while thinking, "Well, isn't this is going to be a crappy day!"

Then I catch myself: whoa, whoa, whoa. Get a grip, Ida! Are you seriously going to let this ruin a perfectly good day? Charlie's right—it's just a bowl, for God's sake. You can find another one on eBay. And the potato salad is just, well, potato salad. Reset your day, dear. Stop at the Busy Bee on your way and buy some cinnamon rolls, the ones with the maple icing, and no one's gonna miss your salad. I ended up doing just that and, of course, I had a great time. Plus, I had a husband to brag about. It was a good memory.

So now here I am sitting in my car with the heat blasting, the windows open, hot and hotter air whipping all around, when it came to me that is was the same kind of situation. Again, I have two options: I can let this ruin my day or I can reset. Either way, I must deal with the situation so I might as well do it happy as mad.

I drive over to Tiger's Garage, (Where the service is always grrreat!). Tiger's been Tiger for so long, I don't think his own mother knows his real name anymore. Anyhoo, Tiger got right on it, and by chance his girlfriend, Danielle, happened to be droppin' off his lunch, so she was able to give me a ride home. Turns out one of the cooling fans froze. Tiger had to order the part, but on Monday, my car was as good as new. Thank goodness it acted up when it did because later that week, I had to go to Bangor for an eye exam, and if my car started acting funny on that lonesome stretch of road, it would have been scary as all get out.

You know what? That Saturday ended up being a pretty good day, after all. I got most of my errands done, and the ones I didn't weren't that important, anyways. I had some catch-up time at home and was able to dust and reorganize a few drawers.

That evening, Charlie and me had a date night, my treat. I says to him, "I never did thank you proper for being such a good guy when I broke that green bowl. How about I take you out to Bonanza for supper?"

"It's a deal. And if you play your cards right, I'll buy you a Peanut Buster Parfait after."

"Sweet talker."

Follow Your Bliss

The other day, I was visiting my niece Caitlin down to the Mahoosuc Health Food, and I overheard a couple of the regulars talking. This gal's got these Rastaman dreadlocks down to her waist, and the fella's sporting this tattoo of a snake coiled around his neck. Whatever floats your boat, right?

"Hey, Connor!" says Rasta-girl.

"Hey!"

"How's it going?"

"Can't complain. I came in to pick up some of this magic herbal juju for my bonsai. The stuff's epic."

"Cool! That little tree of yours is perfection. You're an artist, my man."

"Thanks! Follow your bliss, right?"

Wow, I'm thinking, I'm all for choosing to be happy, but "Follow your bliss?" Sounds good, but complicated. And if I'm busy following my bliss, how am I going to get all the things done I need to get done? You know, glamorous things like cooking dinner and cleaning the bathroom. Of course, before I follow my bliss, I gotta figure out what the hell my bliss is. And what if I spend my whole life searching, and never find it? That would stink.

> *And if I'm busy following my bliss, how am I going to get all the things done I need to get done?*

That's when I realize the thought of following my bliss is stressing me out.

It's only five letters long, but bliss is a big word for a Mainer. Not really part of our heritage. My grandparents lived long and productive lives, and probably never once thought about following their bliss. We could substitute the word passion, but that's a whole other kettle of fish, the mere thought of which makes many a Mainer a little uncomfortable, to say the least.

"Caitlin!" I says a bit later, "What's this follow your bliss business, anyways?"

"Well, Aunt Ida, to me, follow your bliss means doing something that makes me lose track of time. In a good sort of way."

"Not in a 'went on a binder and blacked out' sort of way," I say.

"Right. It's something that relaxes and recharges me. I stop thinking about life's little irritations, get totally into whatever I'm doing, and completely lose track of time. That's how I feel when I do yoga."

"Then, I guess for me, it's crafts. Time just flies. It's just me and my glue gun, sequins and what not, in the flow, happy as a clam. Come to think of it, it's the same with Charlie and the remote! (Just kidding.) I know he feels the same kinda thing when he's puttering around in his workshop."

"Reading a good book can do it, too," Caitlin adds.

"Or how about reading a good book while taking a hot bath and being spoon fed candied-bacon ice cream by a scantily clad hunk?"

"I don't know, Aunt Ida. That kinda sounds like bliss overload."

"Yeah, but what a way to go!"

What's that thing that makes you lose track of time, in a good sort of way? Whether you call it taking charge of your personal happiness, following your bliss, having a hobby, or going on a mini-vacation from your life, I don't care. Find that thing, and do it at least once a week, though once a day would be better. You'll emerge refreshed and re-energized, and your marriage will the better for it.

Recipe for Romance: Take Yourself On a Date

Once you've found that thing that makes you happy, you must put it in your calendar. That's right—schedule your bliss or it ain't going to happen. Maybe it is just taking a walk and getting your favorite ice cream or eating at your favorite restaurant. How about watching a movie in the afternoon with popcorn? (Live dangerously and say "Yes!" to the chemical-butter-flavored topping.) Or visit an art museum or shop at that special store, you know, the one where they wait on you and really fit you for a new bra. Heck, you could just shut off the phone and computer, pour yourself a cup of tea (or wine) and read a good book. Or maybe rent a hotel room for a night—just you. Wouldn't that be fun? I don't know why they don't run sweetheart deals for one because they should.

The World is My Toaster

Good friendships are an important part of my personal happiness. Yes, Charlie and me are best friends, but I have other best friends, too. I just think it's unfair to you and your mate to expect them to be your everything. That's a lot of pressure. Besides, sometimes you just need to talk about your mate with someone, you know, to blow off some steam. Friends are like a pressure valve; they help keep things on an even keel.

Spending time with the Women Who Run with the Moose makes me happy, and I bring that joy back to my relationship. We have a girls night out once a week. Been doing it for years. Sometimes we'll go shopping in Bangor or take a class, like Zumba, or do some scrapbooking, or just go out to eat.

Like a few weeks back, Celeste, Rita, Betty, Dot, Shirley and me buzz over to the all-you-can-eat-buffet down to the Hukilau Polynesian Restaurant. We love going there, so we were really looking forward to it.

We ordered our usual: a couple of pupu platters, then on to the buffet for egg rolls, fried rice, lo mien, and some kind of meat on sticks (we don't ask questions). The girls split a couple of Scorpion Bowls. I was the DD (designated driver), so I was nursing a wine spritzer.

Have you ever had one of them Scorpion Bowls? It's this ginormous drink, comes in a big, honkin' bowl with fire floating in the middle, and little paper umbrellas all around. I have no idea what's in it, but, Jeesum Crow, it packs a punch!

Since our last visit, the owners had put signs up everywhere, in the lobby, by the register, in the dining room, over the sink in the bathroom, in the stalls, everywhere. The signs read:

SCORPION BOWLS ARE NOT SOUVENIRS. ANYONE CAUGHT TAKING ONE WILL BE PROSECUTED.

Clearly the Hukilau was having a problem.

We made short work of the pupu platters and were chomping our way through the buffet, when Betty asks, "So how many Scorpion Bowls do you have to drink before you start thinking about taking one home?"

"Beats me," replies Dottie, "but we're on our way to finding out!"

Always the practical one, Shirley chimes in, "Okay, say you wanted to take one. How would you smuggle it out?"

"Geesh," I says. "You'd need a pretty big purse."

Betty adds, "Well, you could pretend you were pregnant. Though it's not really the right shape, is it?"

"Yeah," I says, "you'd have to hold it, like the baby was on its way. It'd be tricky."

"Some folks must have figured it out," Celeste says. "I mean, by the number of signs, the Hukilau is in the middle of an epidemic."

Rita pipes up, "You gotta admit, though, having your own Scorpion Bowl at home would be kind of special, you know? You'd feel like, wow, the world is my toaster."

We all stop, and look at her. Rita backpedals. "What are you looking at? I'm not saying I'd take it!"

> *"You gotta admit, though, having your own Scorpion Bowl at home would be kind of special, you know? You'd feel like, wow, the world is my toaster."*

"Rita, it's not toaster," Shirley explains. "The world is not your *toaster*. It's oyster. The world is your oyster."

Rita makes a face.

"Oyster? That doesn't make any sense," she says. "Why would you want the world to be your oyster? They're all gooey and slimy."

"Right," Dottie agrees. "Like someone just hocked up a big . . ."

"Hey!" Shirley shouts. "I'm still eating, here!"

Rita looks positively flabbergasted. "Geesh, my whole life I thought it was, The world is your toaster."

Betty says, "Sound more appealing, doesn't it? A toaster takes something cold and makes it hot."

"Nelson does the same thing to me," adds Celeste, nodding over at the bartender, and we all burst out laughing. Nelson smiles in our direction and we wave.

"I'm thinking about tryin' to steal the Scorpion Bowl," Shirley says. "See if he'll frisk me!"

Nelson comes over to our table.

"You ladies are having too much fun! Can I get you another round?"

"You kidding?" Betty says. "We're halfway under the table as it is."

God, we have a good time! We were still giggling when we climb into the car, each sporting a little umbrella in our hair.

Straight Talk From the Barcalounger: Saran Wrap

We have this one guy at work, his wife calls him every fifteen minutes about nothing. Absolutely nothing. He can never go out for a drink after work or volunteer down to the fire station. She is not sick or anything. She's just demanding as all get out. I remember this one time, bunch of us were going to Portland to a Seadogs game, and we invited him along. I could tell he really wanted to go, but had to check with his wife. That was that. Next day, he comes in and says, "Sorry guys. My wife has me scheduled every weekend until the end of the summer."

I'm thinking, I bet Saran Wrap (that's what we call her, because she's so darn clingy) has the poor guy scheduled from now until Dooms Day. I'm glad Ida's not like that!

It's not like we don't do stuff together. We do. But we're not joined at the hip. My advice? Keep the Saran Wrap where it belongs—in the kitchen drawer.

Love Mahoosuc Mills Style: "How Can I Miss You If You Don't Go Away?"

I was talking to my sister the other day. "What do you have planned for this weekend, Reney?"

"Nothing!" she replies, a big smile on her face. "Jimbo's snowmobiling up to Presque Isle, so I have the whole weekend to myself."

"Oh, that sounds heavenly! What're you gonna do?"

"A whole bunch of nothing, Ida. Binge watch something on Netflix, maybe. Give myself a facial and mani-pedi, if I have the energy. Catch up on my *Oprah* magazines."

"You're killing me! And the menu?"

"Haute cuisine. Popcorn and Junior Mints. That's as far as I got."

"That's a good start. I am totally jealous!"

Greta Garbo had it right: sometimes, you just want to be alone. Not that I don't like spending time with Charlie. I do. And I love hanging out with the Women Who Run With the Moose. Work's good, too. It's fun chatting with folks, keeping up with what's going on. But, you know what? All that takes a lot of energy, and every now and then, I fill up the tank. And that's best done by my lonesome.

I love my own company. Whether it's working on a project in my craft room or sitting down with a good book or video (usually some rom-com Charlie couldn't care less about), I'm perfectly happy being alone. In fact, some of my best alone times are ones where, if you asked me, I couldn't tell you what the heck I did. I just sort of wander around the house, puttering, watching the birds on the feeder, spacing out, totally free-form. No to-do list in sight!

Sure, I'm alone when Charlie's out snow blowing the driveway or if he spends the day volunteering down to the fire department, but there's nothing quite like a weekend where I have the whole double-wide to myself. On such weekends, I might read a trashy novel while taking a hot bath, crank up the heat, eat ice cream for supper, and rekindle my love affair with Netflix. It all just seems so much more delicious if I know he's gone for a couple of days.

But, you know what the best thing is about having a whole weekend alone? Knowing Charlie will be home at the end of it. Because, to be honest, by Sunday, I miss the guy. I've even been known to go into his closet and smell one of his shirts. You can wash 'em all you like, but they still smell like him. On Sunday, I'll say to Scamp, "Guess who's coming home today? Charlie!" I might cook one of his favorite dinners or make him some cookies or something. And Scamp's no dummy. As the day progresses, I see him going to the window, looking out.

"Charlie should be here any minute, little buddy. Do you hear his truck?" When he drives up and walks through the door, I'm happy to see him and Charlie's happy to see me, too. In fact, we're both kind of refreshed from our time apart.

Let's face it: when you're with each other 24/7, conversation can get a little thin. Being apart gives us something to talk about when we come back together. And God knows, after forty years of marriage, that's a good thing.

The Honey Do List

Now let's say Charlie stays home alone and I'm the one who goes away for the weekend, I don't think he misses me at all because he's so busy getting things done. Charlie's a doer. I'm lucky that way. We are both doers, really.

However, when it comes to chores, we go our separate ways. I'm not into this "let's share all the housework" stuff. We tried that once when we first got married, and it was awful. We set aside a Saturday morning and divided up the stuff that needed to be done. I dusted and cleaned the bathroom. Charlie vacuumed and tidied up the kitchen. Well, that was the theory anyways. What we ended up with was a poorly cleaned house and lots of bad attitude. Not just from Charlie because he didn't want to do housework, but from me, thinking he was doing a terrible job.

I'm not into this "let's share all the housework" stuff. We tried that once when we first got married, and it was awful.

And that was that. From that day on we took a separate, but equal approach to chores. I say we can't all be quarterbacks. Choose your position on the playing field and do a good job at it. For the most part, I take care of the inside of the house: cleaning, grocery shopping, and cooking. Charlie takes care of the outside: shoveling snow, raking the leaves, and mowing the lawn.

There's a little crossover. We do the dishes and pay bills together. Charlie takes care of any inside repairs or emergencies (plugged toilet, leaky faucet). I plant the annuals, tend to the potted plants, and do a little weeding from time to time. But by and large, the house is my department and the yard is Charlie's. He's got one of them zero-turn mowers that he just loves. Has a shed with a ramp he keeps it in.

Oh, and I come up with a punch list of bigger things that need to be done—Charlie's "Honey Do" list. I'm very good at that; I guess you could say it's my specialty. And he doesn't complain, God bless him. Actually, I think Charlie's better with a list of chores he can cross off. So long as he sticks to my list, he's great. And Charlie's always proud of what he's accomplished. Trouble comes when he starts improvising like he did awhile back with a boot brush. More on that later.

You could be at it all day, dusting, vacuuming, cleaning the bathroom, and washing knickknacks, curtains, and rugs. You may have even cleaned out a bookcase and organized the catch-all drawer. He'll walk in and go, "What's for supper?"

That's it.

"Ida, I moved that little lilac like you wanted."

Even if I'm in the middle of something, I go outside and do some appreciating. That's perhaps the most important part of any Honey Do list, and don't you forget it. Your task as the maker of the list is to tell him what a great job he did. Oh, and don't forget to say thank you. Throw in one of his favorite meals, and you're golden the next time you ask him to do something else around the house.

Now, this appreciation is not an automatic vice-versa kind of thing, unfortunately. After a day of vigorous housecleaning, your husband is probably not going to come home and start admiring all your handiwork. It just ain't gonna happen. It's not that he doesn't care; it's just that he doesn't notice. You could be at it all day, dusting, vacuuming, cleaning the bathroom, and washing knickknacks, curtains, and rugs. You may have even cleaned out a bookcase and organized the catch-all drawer. He'll walk in and go, "What's for supper?"

That's it.

Don't waste your time and energy gettin' mad at him. It's just a fact of life. The thing is, you have to tell him what you've done, and in some cases, show him. "Honey, come see the catch-all drawer!"

Once you point out all the hard work you've been doing, if he's worth his weight in salt, he'll go, "Thank you," or "That looks great, honey!" Which is your opening to say, "I thought we'd go out to dinner. How about a DQ burger and some onion rings? Maybe even split a brownie sundae for dessert?"

Needless to say, that kind of evening is a lot more fun than the alternative. You know what I'm talking about. After a day of housecleaning and your husband not noticing all your hard work, you spend the evening banging and slamming things in the kitchen as you get dinner ready. Or moping around the house, staring forlornly into space, sighing, giving him the silent treatment.

Take pity on him, and yourself. In a world where so many things are out of our control, this, for heaven's sake, is doable. Take time to appreciate your husband, and point him in the right direction so he can appreciate you. Take charge of your personal happiness.

Getting Goin'

- Next time you experience another FGO (Friggin' Growth Opportunity), commit to trying the Not a Crappy Day Option rather than getting mad.
- What makes you lose track of time, in a good sort of way? Could be reading, knitting, walking the dog, or gardening. Doesn't have to be complicated or highfalutin. Block out some time to do it at least once a week, even once a day, if you can manage it.
- Take yourself on a date. I mean, don't just think about it. Plan it. Schedule it. Do it.
- Make a standing date with a friend. If you wait to schedule it until you're ready to see her, it'll be another few weeks before you can fit each other in.
- Put appreciation at the top of your Honey Do List, and give your spouse the opportunity to do the same by telling (or showing) him what you've done.

Four

Sex? I'm in Favor Of It

Sex?

I'm in favor of it. In fact, it's my favorite contact sport.

A while back, me and the girls went to give blood. We try to do this every now and then because it's a good thing to do. Plus, they give you snacks after, so it's a win/win. They also ask you a ton of personal questions, which can take a little getting used to.

So afterward, we're sitting in the recovery area, drinking juice and eating Cheez-Its and Oreo cookies like we were going to jail, when Celeste says, "How about those questions, huh? Shirley, what did you say when they asked about having sex with a gay man?"

"I told 'em that was kind of personal, but if they really needed to know, yes, as far as I can tell, when my husband and me are having sex, he seems happy."

At which point, we go into hysterics.

And there you have it folks. Sex is easy to joke about, but hard to talk about. Even with your friends. Even with your mate.

Certainly, with your kids. You might fantasize about doing it with a movie star or the UPS guy, but generally, we don't like to think about people knowing each other in the biblical sense. Does anyone? I mean I don't want to think about Sadie Dupris, our town librarian, and her husband Frank, who's an accountant, engaged in a torrid exploration of the Dewey Decimal system. No thank you. Or, God forbid, think about Whitey and June Herbert getting intimate on one of them blue tarps they use to cover the tables at their permanent yard sale. Geez Louise, I may have to poke out my eyes after that last picture flashed into my mind!

But, this is a book about marriage, and sex is part of the equation. So I'm just gonna give it a go.

Tippy Canoe and Ida, too

We celebrated Dot and Tommy's fortieth wedding anniversary last July with a big blow-out up to their camp. We had lobsters and steamers, coleslaw, macaroni salad, corn on the cob, ambrosia (I brought that), and homemade biscuits. And desserts? Oh, Mister Man! Don't know if I was more buzzed by the sweets or the sugar-free Jell-O shots (gotta save calories where we can)!

Oh, and Junior made his famous bean hole beans. Ever had 'em? It's a guy thing because, you know, it involves digging a hole, filling it with old tire chains, and playing around with fire for the better part of three hours. The woman helps out a bit, preppin' the beans. Then the guy buries the bean pot in the fire pit, where it stays all night, cooking away. Next day, the guy digs the pot out. Man, are those beans ever tasty!

All the usual suspects were there: Celeste and Bud, Rita and Smitty, Betty and Pat, Dot and Tommy (of course), Shirley and Junior, and me and Charlie. Shirley and Junior went up Friday, so they could get the beans started. The rest of us arrived the next morning. We told Dot and Tommy not to get there until the afternoon. We didn't want them lifting a finger to help.

Betty and me made a special trip to the party store in Bangor for supplies. Side note: have you ever noticed that the people who work at the party store aren't exactly the life of the party? I mean, this little glum gal greeted us when we walked in the door. "Welcome to The Party Place," she says, in a monotone voice with zero energy. It got Betty and me to giggling, it was so ridiculous.

Anyhoo, we flirted with doing a luau theme because we like them leis. But we weren't up for roasting a pig, and it would be hard to get one of them apples in a lobster's mouth! So we went with pink flamingos. Nothing says Maine like pink flamingos, right? We got pink flamingo plates and a pink flamingo table cloth, pink and green plastic cups, balloons and streamers, little pink flamingo party favors, and a few big ones to decorate the yard. We thought we were done, then Betty noticed pink flamingo temporary tattoos. Some things were just meant to be!

> *We thought we were done, then Betty noticed pink flamingo temporary tattoos. Some things were just meant to be!*

What a blast we had decorating that camp! We even gussied up the pontoon boat, which we call the party boat. Why? 'Cause it is. That night, we pile in, take the boat out to the middle of the lake. There, we swapped stories like only old friends do, you know? Because it was an anniversary party, these stories had a kind of lovey-dovey theme to 'em.

Junior told the one where he and Shirley were necking up to Makeout Point, and he forgot to put the parking brake on. Into the bushes they went. And Celeste told the one where she and

Bud went camping and somehow managed to pitch their tent in a cow field and the cows kept waking them up, licking their tent.

"Remember the time Charlie and Ida went out in a canoe for the night."

"Oh, no," mumbles Charlie.

"Yes!" Dot replies. "How could we could we ever forget that canoe trip!"

Everyone laughs and nods their heads.

"I don't think we have to go into that one again," I say.

"Refresh my memory," Tommy asks, like he's clueless. "What exactly happened?"

Betty goes, "I think it was someone's anniversary."

"Or Fourth of July," adds Bud. "It was some hot, as I recall."

"Doesn't matter," Pat replies. "Let's just say it was a long time ago. The kids were little, all bunked down in the loft.

"So it's time to go to bed, right? And we're discussing sleeping arrangements, flipping a coin to see who gets a bed and who's slumming it in the tent.

"'That's okay,' says Charlie, 'Me and my sweetheart'll sleep in the canoe.' "

"Seemed like a good idea at the time," Charlie quips.

"To be honest," I add, "it kinda took me by surprise, but I figured, What the heck?"

Shirley goes, "Well, I don't blame you. Charlie *was* lookin' a little frisky that night." And everybody chuckles.

"Geez, that canoe can't have been too comfortable," Betty chimes in.

"Where there's a will, there's a way," and Charlie winks at me.

"Probably like doin' it on a water bed," Rita says. "I hated ours. Kinda made us seasick, huh, Smitty?"

"Yeah," goes Smitty, "once we set sail!"

Again, much laughter all around the room.

I'm thinking we're on to another story, but Pat picks it up again. "So back to Tippy Canoe and Ida, too! The next morning, dawn's breaking, heads are splitting, and Charlie and Ida are out in the middle of the lake, in a canoe, naked. Right Ida?"

There was no turning back now, so I picked up my cue, "It's quiet, but I hear the engine of a boat drawing near. 'Charlie!' I whisper, 'wake up!'

"Charlie peaks over the edge of the canoe and sees a boat coming fast. 'Ida, put on your life vest. Quick!'

'But what about my clothes?'

'No time. Maybe they won't notice.'"

"Won't notice?" Shirley jumps in, and everybody laughs.

"I'm thinking, 'Wow, this life vest is a lot looser without clothes.' Then I notice poor Charlie struggling to get his on. That's when I realize in our rush to put 'em on, I ended up with Charlie's and him with mine.

"But there's no time to switch, because the boat is right on us. we sat down and put our hands in our laps. Turns out, it was the game warden. What's his face?"

"Gus," goes Tommy. "Gus Turner. Or Tobey Roy."

"It was Gus," Charlie says. "I still remember the look on his face. 'You folks, okay?' he asks."

"'Oh, yes, officer,' I says. 'Just out for an early mornin' paddle.'"

> "Ida was cool as a cucumber, like canoeing buck naked except for your life vest was an every day thing," says Charlie.

"Ida was cool as a cucumber, like canoeing buck naked except for your life vest was an every day thing," says Charlie.

"Gus doesn't skip a beat. Still no smile. 'Didn't see anyone in the canoe. I wanted to make sure it hadn't drifted away from a dock.'

"No, no," I says, "we're fine. Just getting a jump start on the day!"

" 'Musta been in a hurry,' he said."

No one says anything.

"I think I might of seen a flicker of a smile on Gus's face, 'Glad to see you're takin' safety precautions, but you might want to switch up those vests. Charlie's is looking a tad small.' And vroom, off he goes. And none too soon, either, because I felt a giggling fit coming on."

"God, did we bust a gut, huh, Ida? How could you not? 'Glad you're taking safety precautions.'"

"I got to laughing so hard, would have peed my pants . . . "

" . . . if you was wearin' any!"

We're all chuckling as someone segues into another story and another. After awhile, though, we piped down and just sat there, gazing at the stars and listening to the loons. That's about as good as it gets here in Maine.

We all stayed over, though not in the canoe. Celeste and Bud had brought up their camper, which sleeps four. Rita and Smitty pitched their tent and the rest of us bunked down inside.

The next morning, them loons didn't sound so magical to those of us who woke with a big head. We had leftover beans and biscuits for breakfast, and Dottie fried up a whole mess o' bacon. Along with good strong coffee, some of the guys had what they refer to as barley juice for breakfast. (Any other time of day, we call it beer.)

While the boys went fishing, us gals tidied up. We had leftovers for lunch and headed home, temporary tattoos still in place.

Warm Up, Cool Down

Now I have to confess, that canoe incident was many moons ago, and Charlie and me just aren't that motivated anymore. Don't get me wrong. We still enjoy an intimate encounter, but we're just not willing to put our backs out to do it. You watch movies and television shows and they're always jumping at each other, can't get their clothes off fast enough. Ripping the buttons off perfectly good shirts and blouses, thongs in shreds (not that there's much to shred). They're walking backwards toward the bedroom, necking all the while and not paying attention to where they're going. Sexy? No, it's a recipe for disaster. And when they're going at it up against the wall when there's a perfectly good bed a few feet away. I'm thinking, "How exactly does that work? Aren't his legs getting tired?" Or worse: the couple is doing it on the stairs. Oh, my aching back!

> *And when they're going at it up against the wall when there's a perfectly good bed a few feet away. I'm thinking, "How exactly does that work? Aren't his legs getting tired?"*

When I was younger and on a fitness kick, you know what I hated most? The warm up and cool down. If I was taking a class, or doing an exercise video at home, I'd usually skip it all together. Just seemed like a waste of time.

Funny how things change. Now, my favorite parts of working out are the warm up and cool down. I actually like slowly waking up my body and easing into it. And I love cooling down, leaning into the stretches, and thanking my body for being there for me.

At this point, it's the same with my day in general, and sex in particular. It's more pleasurable when we take the time to properly warm up and cool down.

Gels? Yes. Pills? Yes. Mirrors? No. Trapeze? I think not!

I ran into a gal (who shall remain nameless) down to the A&P a while back, and we're chatting away about this and that and she says she's into a redecorating project.

"Oh really, which room?" I ask.

"We're turning our spare room into his man cave, as he calls it, Ida. You know, it's good for him to have a space to call his own."

"Plus it gives you both some breathing room. I don't know who loves Charlie's workshop more, me or him?"

"I hear you," she said. "I took care of a fresh coat of paint and the curtains, leaving him free to concentrate on the important stuff. Oh, he's got the thing all decked out—flat screen TV, computer, recliner, and his bed, of course. We sleep in separate rooms now, because he snores something fierce."

At this point, I'm thinking, we all snore. Man up. As I said earlier, I'm all for sleeping apart if one of you is sick, but this separate rooms thing is a stretch for me. I mean, it's hard to get a fire going if the kindling is in the other room.

Fact of life: as we get older, things change in the sex department. You may need to make more of an effort than you did before to get started. It's a matter of planning vs. spontaneity. If you can wrap your head around that, you're more than half way there. (This will help you if you have kids, too.)

I'm not saying you have to put sex on the calendar (though that might not be a bad idea). Just don't let too much time pass between rolls in the hay. Rule of thumb: if you're starting to snip at each other for no real reason, feeling a little distant, unloved and unloving, try to remember the last time you had fun between the sheets? Can't remember? Time to make a play date.

Chapter 7 is dedicated to dating your mate, so we don't have to get into it here. Let's just jump to the intimate part of your evening or morning or afternoon. Hey, whatever floats your boat!

Men and women have different needs and speeds in the sex department (what else is new?). After a certain age, your window of opportunity gets smaller. It's a fine balance. You need enough time for the woman to get interested, but not so much time that the man loses steam.

Here's where it might be nice to have a talk with your doctor. They're making advances in this department all the time, so if you tried something a while back and didn't like it, ask again. They may have a new approach. Nothing to be embarrassed about. In fact, it's a loving thing to do, and shows your commitment to your relationship. This works best if you both pitch in. Pills for him plus gels for her, equals a good time for both.

Remember to savor the warm up and cool down. Especially if you've been together awhile. Gently allow your body to wake up. Give yourself the luxury of easing into it. And après "date," take time to think about how thankful you are to still love each other this way. Enjoy that afterglow. Not just right then, but the next day and the next. Being intimate with someone you love is a gift. Honor it!

Astro Turf Nightie

Is your husband so into sports, you're thinking about wearing an astro turf nightie to get his attention? If you can't beat 'em, join him because I know from personal experience that watching a contact sport with your mate, can lead to more contact in the bedroom.

In Chapter 2, I talked about finding a project you can do while sitting in the same room when your guy is watching the game. Just a little somethin' somethin' to keep you occupied, while you're spending time together.

Or you can take a different approach altogether, and actually watch the game with him. Some of you already do this, so you know what I'm talking about. For the rest of us, this can be kind of radical. But, if intimacy (which you and me know is more than just bumping your private parts together) is what you want, it may be worth the effort. You'll start sharing something he loves with him and that strengthens your bond. I don't know about you, but if I have to choose, I'd rather relax in the comfort of my own den for a few hours with some snacks and a Moxie, flipping through a magazine with a game on TV, than sit in a deer stand with a loaded gun, gnawing on beef jerky, and freezing my butt off at the crack of dawn. But, hey, maybe that's just me.

This is gonna be more fun if you understand the ins and outs of the game you're watching. The more you know, the more interesting it'll be. Choose one sport (you don't want him to get spoiled), and commit to it. I do football. It mostly happens in the fall on Sunday afternoons or Monday nights, so it doesn't conflict with anything much. And yes, I know it's kind of violent, but hockey is worse. It has to be one of those two, because I realized early on I enjoy watching sports more when I can't see the guys faces. It just breaks my heart when someone misses a foul shot or strikes out. But with a helmet on, they're kind of anonymous, which is easier on me emotionally. I also like it because the Patriots

> *It just breaks my heart when someone misses a foul shot or strikes out. But with a helmet on, they're kind of anonymous, which is easier on me emotionally.*

usually do pretty good, and then Charlie's happy and we can celebrate. Plus, whether the Pats are in it or not, there's the Super Bowl, which is a fun party day.

It's easy to learn the basics of whichever game you choose. Especially with the computer. The *Football for Dummies* website has a great cheat sheet where they break it down for you and give you the basic rules, positions, etc. They have 'em for all the sports. For the more intricate plays, you can ask your spouse. Before you know it, you'll be yelling things at the tube, and throwing around terms like touch back and tight end.

 ## Love Mahoosuc Mills Style: Fore Play

When I asked my friend Betty what she thought the key to a happy marriage was, she replied, "Golf."

"Come again?"

"You heard me, golf."

"I'm gonna need a little more information."

"Well, golf is a hobby that we do together. We're outside, having fun. We joined the couples league and have little shindigs with them every once in a while. Sometimes we go away for a golfing weekend. It's like a mini-vacation, because we're not thinking about anything else while we're playing, and so we're kinda just being ourselves."

"I feel like that when we go away on vacation," I say. "I always know I love Charlie, but when we get away together, I remember what I like about him. We laugh and joke around, all relaxed."

"Exactly!"

"Like a few years back, I remember we'd been home from vacation for a couple of days and we got into a little argument about something or other. I says to Charlie, 'Where is the fun-loving guy I was on vacation with?' And he goes, 'I expect he's with the easygoing gal I was on vacation with.'"

"Too funny, but oh, so true!" Betty says. "One time, me and Pat were up to Bethel for a golfing weekend. We'd played eighteen holes, both of us really on our game, had a delicious dinner. So we're back in our room at the hotel, and Pat's "being nice to me," when the fire alarm goes off. We have to stop what we're doing, get all dressed. Out we go, down three flights of stairs . . . "

"Because you're not supposed to use the elevator during a fire."

"Right. We're outside for about five or ten minutes when we get the okay. Alright, back we go to the room. You'd think that would've put a damper on things, but it was kind of exciting and we were still a little jacked up. So Pat's still being nice to me, when I'll be darned, the fire alarm goes off again. Pat doesn't skip a beat, if you know what I'm saying. He just looks at me and says, 'Let it burn, Betty. Let it burn!'"

Gothic Romances

As I said before, I believe we are responsible for our own personal happiness. This is true in the sex department, too. Having a good sexual relationship with yourself keeps things flowing, so everything's in working order when you need it. This can be a hands-on sort of thing, reading a Gothic romance, watching a romantic movie or something. It's nice to have a day dream thing going in your mind. It perks you up and makes you feel kind of sexy. I don't know about you, but I am always younger, cuter, thinner, smarter, richer, multi-lingual, have great clothes, and sport beautiful flowing hair in my fantasies. Hey, it's my party, baby, I can dream if I want to!

There are a few of rules when it comes to fantasies. First off, make sure they take place in your head and not in real life. That's not a fantasy. That's an affair.

Second, Gothic romances and such are fine, but you gotta understand, no man can live up to that day in and day out. If you're expecting that kind of "love at first sight, he can read my mind and knows exactly what to do" fireworks, you're gonna be disappointed. And pretty soon, you'll start taking it out on your mate by being snippy or by spending all your time reading about romance instead of having it. That is gonna do nothing for your personal happiness in the long run.

The final rule when it comes to fantasies, and I can't stress this enough—make sure they don't feature someone you see on a regular basis. That could get creepy or, at the very least, distracting as all get out.

Special Delivery

My friend Rita works down to Smitty's Hardware, which is owned by her husband, Smitty. She's worked at Smitty's since she married him, and you wouldn't believe the stuff she knows. It always surprises me when I go in there and see Rita in action because she's this little wisp of a thing, always dolled up. She doesn't look like she could put gas in her car. And yet there she is talking to Bobby Franceour about shut-off valves and connectors. Or Cy Thibedeau's rewiring his house and he's asking Rita's advice on how to go about it. She goes on about circuits and volts and running cables and I don't know what all.

Of course, it's not easy working with your husband like that, but they've managed it for forty years. I think it's because she works out front, and he's mostly out back or doing deliveries.

Now, I'm pretty good with numbers, so along with my job cashiering down to the A&P, I moonlight doing books for the Mahoosuc Mills Mainely Maine store and Smitty's. So I'm always in and out of the hardware store.

A few years back, I noticed that Rita wasn't quite herself at work. She seemed pretty good when we was hanging out with the Women Who Run With the Moose, but at the store, she was a little distracted. And she started making mistakes on the register (lots of void slips in the cash drawer) and misplacing stuff.

One day, I happened to catch her alone in the break room. "Rita, what's up? You don't seem quite yourself and I'm worried about you."

She looks around, real guilty, and says, "I can't talk about it here, Ida, but I gotta tell someone. Meet me at the Busy Bee tomorrow morning at eight."

Well, that piqued my interest. So the next morning, there I am at the Busy Bee, eight sharp. In comes Rita, dressed cute as ever, but looking a little tired. We each order a bottomless cup of coffee, one of Babe's homemade cinnamon rolls with maple icing and a side of bacon because everything is better with bacon.

We make small talk until our food arrives. It's hard to have a big conversation on an empty stomach. Once we tuck into breakfast, I give Rita a nudge, "Okay, Rita. Something is going on. Spill it!"

"Oh, Ida, I don't really know how to say it."

"Try."

"I'm having an affair."

"Oh, my, God, Rita! With who?"

"Ian."

"Ian who?"

"Ian, the UPS guy."

"You're sleeping with the UPS guy?"

"Yes! Not in real life, of course. I mean, where would I find the time? But I might as well be. I daydream about him all the time."

"Oh, thank goodness! You had me worried for a minute, Rita. That's not an affair. That's a fantasy."

"Technically, yes, but it's taking over. I'm so distracted at work, waiting for him to arrive. Then, I'm all hyper after he leaves. Ian's just so darned cute and polite, and so strong lifting all those boxes."

"You're sleeping with the UPS guy?" "Yes! Not in real life, of course. I mean, where would I find the time? But I might as well be. I daydream about him all the time."

"I hear you. When I got addicted to the home shopping network a few years back, I gotta say, my heart started to go pitter pat at the very sight of our UPS guy. His name was Johnny. I couldn't wait to see the size of the package he was delivering, which sounds kinda dirty, but you know what I mean."

"I knew things were bad when I bought Smitty a brown shirt and some brown pants, and suggested he wear 'em together. I figured if I squinted, he might look like Ian."

"Oh, that is bad. What are you gonna do?"

"Nothing. I'm hoping Ian gets transferred or something."

"These things usually pass. You can move it along, though, by finding a replacement fantasy. But make it someone on TV or in a movie or something. In the meantime, I have a couple of Gothic romances in my car. They might do the trick."

A while later, I realized things at Smitty's had settled down, and Rita seemed like her old self again. I pulled her aside, "How's Ian?"

"Ian who?" she says, smiling.

"What happened? Did you find a replacement?"

"Not yet. But see, one day last week, Ian came in per usual, and I'm all a flutter. He makes his delivery. Once he's back in his truck, I wander over to the window, real casual, for a parting look, and there he is in the truck, talking on his cell phone and picking his nose. I mean, really going at it. Well, that popped the bubble right quick."

Straight Talk From the Barcalouger: Is it Worth it?

Hey, we've all had to chance to stray, whether it's with someone you work with or that cute little waitress when you're off on a snowmobile trip. But you gotta ask yourself: Is it worth it? Am I willing to risk all I have for a half hour of fun and a boat load of guilt? And there's no guarantees in the fun department, either. It's not like you're going to be spending the night in a five-star hotel with a Victoria's Secret model acting out every fantasy you've ever dreamed of.

If you find yourself thinking the grass is greener over there, take a hard look at your own lawn, mister. Does it need tending? Then roll up your sleeves and get to work.

Recipes for Romance: Valentine's Day

I'm writing this the day before Valentine's, if you can believe it. Not only that, it falls on a Saturday, so you know the restaurants are going to be even more packed than usual. Not all that romantic, so I'm thinking of skipping the Valentine's Day "special menu" (code for we've jacked up our prices because it's a holiday).

So what are me and my sweetie gonna do? Well, I saw they were running a Valentine's Day special down to Mikey's Meat Market—shrimp cocktail, filet mignon, risotto, and asparagus, with chocolate-covered strawberries for dessert. Plus, they throw in some Belgian beer (never had it, but it sounds exotic). All I have to do is heat it up and serve. (It's not a holiday if I have to spend too much time in the kitchen.) I'm picking it up early so we can have the shrimp cocktail for lunch. It's hard to feel frisky if you're stuffed to the gills, so we need to pace ourselves.

I'm gonna set the table with the good china, light some candles, and put on some Elvis love songs. After dinner, we'll kick back in our love seat, hold hands and watch a movie, something with a high hunk factor for me and enough action to keep Charlie interested. Then, hopefully we'll continue the celebration in the bedroom. If not, maybe we will the next day or the next. No pressure. This isn't reality TV; it's real life.

Sometimes the most romantic thing you can do is just hang out together, enjoying each other's company, no big deal. Why wait for Valentine's Day?

Hugs and Kisses

Sex is important in a relationship, sure. But affection is key. That's what I miss most if Charlie's away for a long weekend Ski-Dooing or hunting. I miss holding hands. I miss kissing.

Charlie and me always kiss each other good-bye and hello. It worked for my parents, and it works for us. If I'm getting dressed in the morning and Charlie's ready to leave for work, he'll come into the bedroom and kiss me good-bye. When he

gets home from work, I stop what I'm doing (usually fixing supper) and kiss him hello.

Think about it. Which is more appealing: yelling "Good-bye!"
as you're going out the door and your spouse yelling back, "Have
a nice day!" or having a small moment of connection when
you're coming and going. It says, "You're important to me."

Gettin' Goin'

- Have things changed in the sex department? Maybe
  it's time to have a chat with you doctor. Nothing to be
  embarrassed about. In fact, it's a loving thing to do, and
  shows your commitment to your relationship.
- Perk things up with a change of scenery. Even if it's just
  for a weekend, getting away from your everyday routine
  and pressures might be just what you need to get things
  flowing again.
- You are responsible for your own personal happiness.
  Renew your sexual relationship with yourself. No need to
  get into detail here. You know what to do.
- Buy some nice underwear. It's hard to feel sexy in worn
  out granny panties. And while you're at it, buy some new
  underwear for your husband, too. He doesn't care about
  it, but you do.
- Don't wait for Valentine's Day. Plan a romantic evening
  together, whatever that means to you.
- Kiss each other hello and good-bye for a week, and see
  what happens.

Five

When is a Bargain a Bargain?

Yes, this chapter is about money. But if you're looking for advice on how to invest your hard-earned cash, you've come to the wrong place. I'm going to share ways to approach money on a day-to-day basis, things that have worked for Charlie and me. Some of it we've been doing since we got married, and some we had to learn the hard way. I want to save you some pain.

I've heard that rich people find it kind of tacky to talk about money, but for the rest of us, well, we gotta. I'm not saying you need to hash it out every morning, noon, and night, but you and your spouse need to be on the same page. Otherwise, it can be the one thing that does you in.

To Buy or Not to Buy?

When Charlie and me first got married neither of us were making much money. I worked down to the A&P, of course, and Charlie worked at the mill. He's a foreman there now, but he started out at the bottom of the ladder. We had a cute little apartment in town. Our parents helped us out, giving us furniture that they didn't want anymore and my Aunt Alma's old melmac dishes. It was hard, but we made ends meet. I kept my eyes peeled for deals at the A&P. We paid our bills, and had a little left over at the end of the week for a date night. Nothing too extravagant: maybe a couple of beers and a burger, a bean supper down to the Congo Church, or an ice cream sundae. We didn't have much money, so there wasn't much to talk about, right?

Well, there was a big shindig coming up in town. Mahoosuc Mills was celebrating its 150-year anniversary. There was a bunch of stuff going on that summer, but the main event was the Anniversary Ball. It was going to be held at the brand new Sky Lodge (formerly Makeout Point) and serve as their grand opening. They even had a big band comin' up from Portland for the affair. It was going to be a night to remember! The whole town was jacked up about it, and us girls were beside ourselves planning what we were going to wear.

It was a once-in-a-lifetime occasion, right? So Celeste, Rita, Betty, Dot, Shirley, and me decided that we needed to shop for new dresses someplace special—Ward Brothers in Lewiston. That was the swankiest shop around. They had the latest fashions and wonderful sales people who waited on you and everything.

Well, long story short, I fell in love with this dress: crimson red, strapless, sequins on the fitted bodice, nice full skirt, and a little bolero jacket. Oh, my God, was it ever gorgeous, and it fit like a glove! The price tag, however . . . ugh! It cost more than twice what I'd budgeted. But the girls were eggin' me on, saying how beautiful I looked in it, and the sales woman had been so nice. How could I not buy it, right?

As I'm writing the check, though, I started feeling kind of queasy. There were no returns on dresses like this one, only store credit. It was a lot of money to spend on a dress. But oh, what a dress!

When I got home, I 'fessed up to Charlie. That was hard because once the girls and me left the store, the glow of my new dress quickly began to fade. I give Charlie credit; he didn't get mad, though it'd probably have been easier on me if he had. He agreed it was a beautiful dress, and he could see how important it was to me. Now we just had to figure out how to make ends meet for the rest of the month. That was sobering! It was a long couple of weeks eating macaroni and cheese, spam, canned soup, and saltines. I even think we invited ourselves once or twice for dinner at our parents' houses. Somehow, we squeaked by.

In the end, it was worth it. Charlie and me had a great time at the Anniversary Ball, and I felt like a princess in that dress. More importantly, though, I learned a valuable lesson—in a marriage, financial decisions you make effect both of you. That's why, ever since that day, Charlie and me have a couple of rules regarding big purchases. First, we discuss all the pros and cons. Second, we sleep on it and make sure we still feel good about our decision the next day. Sure, it takes impulse buying out of the equation, but we're not talking about a pack of Jujubes here. We're talking about stuff like a new car, gas grill, lawn mower, or heck, a brand new toaster oven or microwave. From our point of view, talking about money is not tacky—it's essential.

> *It was a long couple of weeks eating macaroni and cheese, spam, canned soup, and saltines.*

I certainly know if I'd discussed that dress with Charlie before hand, and we'd both decided it was a good idea, I wouldn't have felt so bad while serving him Rice Krispies for supper.

The Couple that Pays Together, Stays Together

As I said before, I'm pretty good with numbers and even moonlight doing books for a couple of businesses. So, it would be easy for me to handle all the money stuff at our house. But we all know (or at least suspect) that the easiest course of action isn't always the best. I mean, what happens when the person taking care of the finances gets sick or dies? That leaves the survivor in a bad situation. Not only must they deal with losing a spouse, but they must get up to speed on the money end of things right quick. That's just not fair to either of you.

Remember in Chapter 2, I talked about the importance of showing up? This is the sort of thing I'm talkin' about. You and your mate are in this together. Whether you work outside the home or not, you need to wrap your head around the fact that financial decisions effect both of you. So, both of you need to have a say in what's going where and when.

Charlie and me always sit down and pay bills together. It doesn't take that long. Whether it is monthly or weekly, just put it on the calendar. Usually I open the envelopes, write the amount to be paid in the little boxes and prepare the return envelope. Charlie writes the checks and does the adding and sub-tracting. I double check everything on the check. For credit card or loan payments, we discuss how much we're going to send. You can make this work if you pay bills on the computer, too.

When things were tight (and they have been off and on over the years) this wasn't my favorite thing to do, but fact is, it had to be done. It's easier to deal with things on an ongoing basis, than to let them snowball and struggle to play catch up. Make sure you build in a little fun time after one of these bill-paying sessions. Breakfast down to the Busy Bee usually does the trick for us, or a walk with Scamp. At the very least, give each other a hug. You deserve it!

Love Mahoosuc Mills Style: Gettin' Motivated

The other day in the break room down to the A&P, I'm chatting with my fellow cashier, Liz. She and her husband, Todd, just got back from a cruise. She's telling me all about it. Showing me pictures.

You know how lookin' at pictures of someone else's vacation can be boring as all get out? They usually have my attention for the first few, but then they start saying things like, "This isn't really a great picture, but . . . " Or "This is a couple that we met. They're from blah, blah and he's a blah, blah, blah . . . " Excruciating!

You need to head 'em off at the pass. What I do is say, "Sure, I'd love to see pictures of your trip. Show me your top ten."

Works like a charm with snapshots of grandkids, too.

Anyhoo, Liz showed me her top ten pics, and then she says they already put a down payment on a cruise for next year. I guess they offered them a sweet deal.

"We had the money tucked away in savings anyways," Liz says, "so why not?"

Well, that got my attention because as luck would have it, I was writing this chapter.

"I think of you and Todd as being good with money, Liz . . . "

"Well, I am. Todd, not always."

"So you're not totally in sync in this department?"

"Nope."

"Then do you mind me asking how you go about saving? They say you should pay yourself first. Is that what you do?"

"Well, not exactly. A few years ago, when Todd got laid off, that was tough. We really didn't have enough put away for emergencies, and it was kind of scary."

"I'll bet."

"After that, I decided to start what I call the cover-our-butts fund. I was determined to have a buffer if we needed it, so I started putting money in every week. Not much, but a little."

"Every bit helps, right?"

"It sure does. After a while, it started to build up."

"Did you have a big discussion with Todd about it?"

"Not really. I just knew I needed to feel secure in order to be happy, so I was doing what I needed to do for my peace of mind."

"Good for you!"

"I told Todd about it, of course. And left it at that."

"Did he hop on board?"

"Not at first. It was just me all by my lonesome putting money in week after week. Honestly, the hardest part of the whole thing was trying not to feel resentful about him not doing the same. I just had to let it go. Then one day we were talking about upgrading our motor boat to a cabin cruiser, and all of a sudden things changed. Todd started putting money into the account. Not a little every week, but a big chunk every now and then.

"Turns out just saving for savings' sake didn't motivate him, but having something specific to save for did. Once we got enough money in the account, he could see the advantage of it because instead of putting something big like a new washing machine on a credit card, we could borrow it from ourselves, and pay ourselves back."

"Interesting! You both think of money in different ways, so what motivates you to save is different."

"Yup!"

"I love how you did what you needed to do to feel comfortable, Liz, and eventually, in his own way, Todd got on board."

"Well, I don't know if it was Oprah who said it or what, but, you know, women have to hold the bigger vision for the couple."

"Ain't that the truth!"

Sure It's Ugly, but it Works Like a Charm

The longer I'm married, the more I realize that sometimes men and women have completely different ways of looking at things. What's a priority for you, money wise, may not be a priority for him. And vice versa. So you gotta learn to choose your battles. Easier said than done, right?

Like a few years ago, out of the blue, Charlie says to me, "Ida, you know what we need?"

"A complete kitchen make-over?"

"Smaller."

"A set of Fiestaware?"

"No, a boot brush."

"A boot brush?"

"You know, put it by the door? Has a brush on top? You wipe your boots on it before coming into the house."

"Oh, I've seen those," I said. "You mean like a little porcupine, with a brush on its back?"

"Well, I don't know about a porcupine. Just your basic boot brush."

> *It looked like a piece of folk art gone horribly wrong. How long, I'm thinking, are we going to have to live with this?*

"Okay, Charlie, I'll look into it. You know how much I love a shopping project."

So, I threw myself into it. See, Charlie's pretty good about wiping his feet when he comes in the door. (Not so much when we first got married, but eventually he came around.) Heck, I'm thinking, anything that'll help keep the house clean is worth searching for. It took awhile, but I finally found one that did the trick, one that both Charlie and me could live with.

It had a nice design on the base (for me), and a kind of rusty finish (for Charlie). Far as he's concerned, the rustier looking the better. It came with a black brush originally, and it worked pretty good for a season or two. It was there by the front door and we both used it, least until the bristles gave out. Then, it got demoted to the shed, and I promptly forgot about it.

Well, last fall, a modified version appeared.

"Charlie, what's up with the boot brush?"

"All fixed."

"I can see that." What the hell? I'm thinking. "Why didn't you just ask me to buy a new one?"

"Oh, it just needed a new brush."

I stare at the thing. Charlie had obviously found some replacement head for a shop broom at the hardware store, and tacked it on. It looked like a piece of folk art gone horribly wrong. How long, I'm thinking, are we going to have to live with this?

"Charlie . . ."

"I know, I know, it's ugly, but it works like a charm." He wipes his boots across the bristles, sending little bits of sand and grit flying. "See? And only $6.95 down to Smitty's."

And there you have it, folks. "It's ugly, but it works like a charm." For a woman, the first part of that sentence cancels out the second. For a man, it's the other way 'round. All I have to say is "bean bag chair," and you know I'm right.

Well, I was fixing to tell Santa we needed a boot brush for Christmas, but Charlie was so proud of his ingenuity, and the fact that he'd only spent $6.95, that I just didn't have the heart to play hard ball. But darn if that thing weren't ugly as all get out!

Eventually, I started hinting around about replacing it. You know, making subtle suggestions, like maybe we could move the boot brush to the back door or off the deck, or by the shed. At first, nothing happened.

Then one day, there the boot brush was, sitting on the deck by the back door. Hallelujah!

"I thought it might work better there," Charlie says.

"Great idea!" And that's where it's been ever since. I see it, but I don't see it, you know? So it doesn't bother me.

Then one Saturday morning this spring, I'm cleaning the kitchen, when out of the corner of my eye I see Charlie measuring something on the deck. He's going back and forth to his shop, moving with purpose. Didn't think nothing of it until I hear the screw gun—then the penny drops—Oh, God! My husband's doing some sort of construction project without my supervision. This can't be good!

"Charlie, what are you doing?"

"The boot brush was moving around too much when I wiped my feet, so I added these wooden stops. This way, it'll stay put."

> *Didn't think nothing of it until I hear the screw gun, then the penny drops—Oh, God! My husband's doing some sort of construction project without my supervision. This can't be good!*

I stand there, stunned. Somehow, he'd managed to make the darn thing even uglier.

Charlie takes my shocked silence as admiration, "Clever, huh?"

"Wicked."

"I'll paint it when I do the deck."

Then all proud, he steps back and goes, "Ida, give it a shot."

And being the good wife that I am, I try brushing my shoes across it. Sure as shooting, it works like a charm.

Recipes for Romance: Having Fun Without Breaking the Bank

All budget and no play makes for a dull life and can put stress on your relationship. If things grow dull, put on your thinking cap, and come up with some fun things to do together that won't break the bank. You know, the whoopie pie isn't the fanciest dessert out there, but it's still pretty darn tasty. Same concept applies here.

Look for restaurant specials in your local paper or online. Maybe you just go out for a pizza and a pitcher of beer or to the Dairy Queen. Heck, McDonalds hot fudge sundaes are inexpensive and pretty darn yummy. Take your sundaes up to the Sky Lodge and park overlooking the lake, and who knows what trouble you could get into. Or instead of going out to dinner, make a breakfast or lunch date. Cheaper, but still fun.

Look for discount coupons or deals for fun things you wouldn't normally try, like tubing or an evening at the arcade. Heck, buy bikes at a yard sale and start riding. Speaking of yard sales, why not spend a Saturday yard saling? There's stuff for both of you to look at. You get the idea. You don't have to spend lots of money to have fun! Get creative!

Bucky's New Boots

I ran into Bucky Dumont down to the A&P one day this winter. He's the fella with the horses who gives sleigh rides during our Down Home Holiday Festival. I was shopping after work, and he was picking up a few things for the missus. Sure enough, there in his shopping cart were milk, sugar, and a dozen eggs.

"How about that case of Pabst, Bucky. She ask you to pick that up?"

"Nope. Them's what I call my office supplies."

I've seen Bucky's office. It's that shed off the barn where he fixes his farm equipment and maintains the horse tack. Oh, he's got it all decked out: ancient pot bellied stove, TV, mini fridge, box of cigars, an old Barcalounger and a rocking chair or two. All, you know, for his buddies, when they drop over for a board meeting. I'm thinking, it's winter, their wives are probably sick of 'em, anyway!

I notice Bucky is wearing a pair of decent looking black boots. Brought me up short, because usually he's in totally beat up old clod hoppers.

"Gee, Bucky, look at those swanky boots!"

"Got 'em down to Mardens. Been trying to break 'em in, but they still smell like old tires."

"I hear you, Bucky. I once got a faux leather jacket down to Reny's that smelled like that. Seemed like a good deal at the time." And it was kind of cute, too, if you ignored the odor.

Experience has taught me, there are some things you can buy cheap, like plastic cups for the deck, and some

Experience has taught me, there are some things you can buy cheap, like plastic cups for the deck, and some things you shouldn't, like a good bra and moisturizer.

81

things you shouldn't, like a good bra and moisturizer. Listen, I'm all for them BOGO sales down to Payless, but I'm not about to buy my work shoes there. I'm on my feet thirty hours a week behind the check out counter, where nobody can see what I'm wearing. So, I'm going for comfort, not looks. But sure, if I see a cute little pair of summer sandals at Payless with polka dots or bows, I'm getting 'em. I know they'll last only one season, if I'm lucky and I don't step in a mud puddle!

General rule of thumb? Put your money into staples. You know, your winter coat and boots, smoke alarms, liquid foundation with all the bells and whistles, under eye concealer (real important), a good piece of meat for dinner, and fresh herbs and spices. Then save money on the flash: scarf, hat, a fun top, lipstick, blush, and eye shadow, cereal, paper towels. Don't skimp on the toilet paper, though. Double-ply all the way.

Anyways, back at the A&P, Bucky goes his way, and I go mine. That's when I become aware of this weird squeaking sound. I'm looking all around. About five minutes later, I hear it again. Just then, Bucky turns to the corner and heads down the aisle toward me. I realize the sound is coming from his direction. At first I thought it was his shopping cart. (You know how that is when you grab a gimpy cart?) But no, it's Bucky's new boots. So not only do his boots smell like old tires, they squeak like all get out when he walks!

"Hello again, Bucky!" I says, eyeing his shopping cart, now plum chucka full of corn chips, pork rinds, Slim Jims and a couple of boxes of day old donuts. "Looks like you got quite a board meeting coming up!"

"Yup," he chuckles. "Solvin' the problems of the world, one beer at a time. It's hard work, but someone's gotta do it."

And off he goes, squeak, squeak, squeak. I'm thinking Bucky's not much of a bargain shopper. Though the "Mrs." probably doesn't mind, because she can hear him coming a mile away!

Straight Talk From the Barcalouger: Get a Professional

When I was younger, I thought I had to do everything around the house myself. Repair the roof, clean the gutters, fix that drippy faucet, you name it. It was a point of pride. Besides, it's always cheaper to do it yourself, right?

Not necessarily. I've learned the hard way that "do it yourself" is sometimes more expensive in the long run. You've got your time factor, of course. How much is your time worth? Then there's the stress and frustration. And you can't forget the cost of gas, because you know it's gonna be a minimum of two trips down to Home Depot. Besides, replacing a toilet is a contact sport I'm just not interested in playing.

Next time something at the house needs fixing, ask yourself if you'd be best calling a professional right off the bat. Take my word for it: costs less for them to fix it first, then to clean up the mess you made of it.

Coupon Intervention

So, I'm working down to the A&P when who do I see get in my register line? Debbie Hunter. My heart sinks. See, it takes forever to cash Debbie out because she always has a ton of coupons. She's organized about it, though, I'll give her that. Has a file folder and everything. Even so, the higher math is above my pay grade and me and my register can't always keep up. And if, God forbid, the coupon doesn't scan the way she wants or she didn't read the fine print, I have to get our manager, Chip, to come over and void it out. That backs up the line, and a cloud of crankiness descends upon whoever is waiting. Not pretty.

But listen, I've worked at the A&P since Moby Dick was a minnow, I know my way around coupons. Since the economy went south, I've seen more and more people using them. Why not save money where you can, right?

Heck, growing up, I still remember my mother filling up her books with them S&H Green Stamps. Remember those? Seems like it took a million of 'em to get a toaster, but she stuck with it.

But this *Extreme Couponing* thing is something else all together. Have you seen that show? Oh, Mister Man, is it ever fascinating, in a watching-a-train-wreck sort of way.

Okay, for all you who haven't seen it, this isn't exactly *Masterpiece Theater*. The show features folks who are so into couponing, that's about all they do. They got whole rooms in their house just filled with stuff they've picked up for next to nothing. I mean, shelves upon shelves of shampoo, dishwashing liquid, boxes of macaroni and cheese, cereal, baby wipes, you name it. It's like they got their very own grocery store.

> *These people haul around ring binders three inches thick, just chock full o' coupons. Really!*

These people haul around ring binders three inches thick, just chock full o' coupons. Really! They buy five or six newspapers a day, then literally spend hours and hours cutting and sorting. For them, a typical shopping trip involves a half day of planning, minimum. Some even suffer from couponing-induced insomnia. I mean, they lie awake at night either thinking about how much they're going to save, or worrying about missing a sale. Some (this is the God's honest truth) even go dumpster diving for coupons. We're not talking homeless people, you understand. These are regular folks like you and me, diving into a dumpster to save a couple of bucks on Hawaiian Punch!

And yes, I know they're getting a good deal on whatever they're buying, but what exactly do you do with nine dozen eggs? Or three bunches of bananas? I mean, come on, folks! They're going to spoil! Oh, I suppose you could make banana bread, maybe for the Band Booster Bake Sale. After all, you got all them eggs. A ton of work, though.

I watch these people and wonder, if you factor in your time, how much money are you really saving? Or, if your goal is to save money, why don't you stop buying stuff and use what you have stockpiled in your garage? Or give some of it to a homeless shelter, or soup kitchen, or something. Heck, maybe they're stockpiling for the Apocalypse, I don't know.

Call me crazy, but isn't it only a hop, skip and jump from *Extreme Couponing* to *Hoarders*? (That's another TV show you can probably miss!)

Anyhoo, it's Debbie's turn at my register.

"Hey, Debbie! How you doing?"

"Okay," she says.

But Debbie didn't seem that way. She looked kind of anxious, beads of sweat on her upper lip. I just thought she was having a hot flash. So, I finish scanning everything, and look at Debbie expectantly. She looks at me, deer in the headlights. Then I notice Debbie doesn't have her file folder.

"Do you have any coupons, Debbie?"

She takes a couple deep breaths. "No, Ida, I don't have any coupons." Debbie starts to tear up, but manages to hold it together.

"Everything alright, Debbie?"

"Sam did a coupon intervention."

"He did?"

"Yup. Said he couldn't take it any more. Wanted his house and his wife back. And I don't blame him. We can't park in the garage anymore, there are so many supplies in it. The spare bedroom looks like a storeroom. Plus, I didn't want to go nowhere or do nothing because I had to keep up with the coupons. It was wearing me down."

"Geez," I says. "What a loving thing for Sam to do. Takes a brave man to stand between a woman and her coupons."

"I know. Still, it's tough. It's the middle of winter, and I don't know what to do with myself."

Gail Perkins, next in line, pipes up. "Gotta keep those hands busy. You need a hobby. Hey, they're offering a knitting class down to the library. That might do the trick. Trudy Lovejoy is teachin' it."

"That's right," I says. "She was in just the other day, putting up flyers."

Debbie muses, "Gee, I've always wanted to take up knitting. And you know, I have a bunch of yarn in the craft section of the garage. Got it down to Michaels last spring. They had a double coupon deal going and I couldn't resist."

"It's like it was meant to be."

There seemed to be a bounce in Debbie's step as she left the A&P. Gail's right. During the winter especially, it helps to keep your hands busy. Cuts down on the calories (if you're like me) and the clutter. Let's just hope, for Sam's sake, Debbie doesn't end up in Knitters Anonymous.

Fun Money

I know a couple in Mahoosuc Mills who are so tight, they squeak when they walk (and they're not wearing Bucky's boots, either). They budget everying down to the penny. And, get this, they account to each other for every single cent. I mean, they buy a pack of Juicy Fruit gum, they get a receipt and fess up. I'm all for having a budget, but that's excessive.

Even with the tightest of budgets, I believe you each need a little fun money to spend without having to justify it to your spouse. We give kids an allowance, and you should have one, too.

It may sound counterintuitive, but having a little fun money actually helps your money situation because it's easier to stick with a budget if you're not feeling resentful about it.

Let's face it, there are times when that pumpkin latte is the only thing that'll get you outta your funk. Guys, you want to get a Bud with the boys or drop by the Busy Bee for a Big Boy Bacon Burger (that's the one they call The Other Woman, because it's so bad for you, you have to sneak to have it). I know it would be hard explain to Charlie why I needed that new Tickle Me Pink nail polish, when I have three other pink nail polishes. But darn, Tickle Me Pink on my toes just perks me up to no end!

Moonlighting

Do you have a hobby or something that you love to do? Is there a way you can use it to pick up a little extra pin money? Like I said before, I moonlight doing books. I wouldn't want to do only bookkeeping, because I like being out in the public, but it's great as a side job. Plus, I enjoy shopping, so the extra money comes in handy.

I don't believe in quitting your day job and trying to make a living with your hobby. Not right away anyways. Making a move like that before your business is ready can put a lot of pressure on the things you love: your family, your lifestyle, and your hobby. Plus, you might turn something you love into just another thing that drags you down. But starting a little side business, building it up (if you want), and slowly cutting back on hours at your day job can be a good way to approach it. Or, like me, you might want to keep it small and manageable. Just a little extra cash on the side. Nothing wrong with that.

Celeste has it down. She's a whiz-bang at chair caning. Loves it! So, she teaches a couple classes a year down to adult ed at Moose Megantic High. Then she picks up extra money finishing the chairs that her students start (because, take it from me, chair caning's not for everyone). She has quite a backlog of chairs in her barn. Celeste calls it "the bank." She works at her own pace, and seems to finish one whenever she needs a little extra cash.

Making some pin money from your hobby is a relationship win/win. There's the money, of course. Plus, you're doing something that you love, which makes you feel good, and you bring that good feeling back to your relationship.

Getting Goin'

- If one of you is not up to speed in the money department, schedule a time to make it happen. It might take more than one session. Plan in some fun time after as a reward.

- Do you pay your bills together? If not, give it a try, even if you each take care of different expenses or if one of you doesn't work outside the house. Before you move on to other things, hug your spouse.
- If you don't have one already, start a cover-our-butts fund.
- Make a list of fun and free (or almost free) stuff to do together. Put in on your fridge for when you need a little inspiration.
- Look for discount coupons and special deals.
- Budget in some fun money for each of you. Even if it's only five dollars a week. You need money you can spend any way you want.
- Do you have a hobby that might generate a little extra money? Go for it. Sign up for a craft fair or put it on Craigslist or Etsy. What do you have to lose?

Six

What Happens in the Double-Wide, Stays in the Double-Wide

I find couples who claim they never argue kind of spooky. A good clean fight every now and then is part of a healthy relationship. Of course, when I say fight, I am not, under any circumstances, refering to actual physical contact. No, I'm talking about arguments that range from little disagreements to heated discussions.

No question, the best kind of argument is the one you don't have because you got a simmering resentment off your chest before it reached a full boil. And it can be fairly simple to do that by actually *talking* with your mate. You know, showing up and asking for what you want.

These two things are particularly important when it comes to compromise, which is key to any successful marriage. You gotta show up with your whole self, assume responsibility for your personal happiness and trust that your mate is gonna do the same. If you both say what you want, you have established a starting point for negotiation. But if you hedge your bets and play your cards close to your chest, trust me, you're gonna get nowhere—except increasingly upset.

We've all probably had this conversation at some point in our relationship: "Where do you want to eat?"

"I don't know. Where do you want to eat?"

"It don't matter to me. Where do you want to eat?"

And it keeps going like this until you're both wicked irritated.

However, instead of waiting for the other person to tell you what they want, try actually saying what you want. (If you don't know, then say what you don't want—I know I don't want pizza or Chinese food, other than that, I'm open.) Then your mate tells you what they do or do not want, and voila! You're on your way to a decision and an argument has been nipped in the bud.

Easier said than done, right? Because sometimes, you don't know what you want or just don't care. Or, even worse, you get miffed about where to eat when you're really upset about something else altogether.

Here's an example of what I'm talkin' about.

The Great Banana Bread Incident

This happened last June, but I remember it like it was yesterday. Charlie and me had a little vacation planned, and I had my heart set on making banana bread for the ride. So the week before we were going to leave, I bought three bananas and set them aside, you know, so they'd be good and ripe to make the bread. That was the plan anyways.

It's not like I didn't tell Charlie, my plan. I was putting the groceries away, and Charlie was doing his famous staring into the fridge, looking for something to eat, but not moving

anything around to see what's really in there routine, when I say
to him, "I'm saving these bananas for banana bread, okay?"

No reply.

"Charlie! I'm saving these for banana bread."

"Heard you the first time."

"Well, honey, sometimes it's hard to tell."

"What do you want to me to do? A cartwheel?"

"No need to be sarcastic. A simple 'okay' or 'yup' would be fine."

Again, nothing. Honest to God! I walk over to the coat closet
door and shut it with a little force. This is another little game
we play. Charlie leaves the door open, and I shut it. As I told
you before, we've been playing this little game forever.

So, back to the banana bread. See, that week was supposed to
be our vacation. We always take off the last week of June to do a
little something special: maybe go up to Dot and Tommy's camp,
take a few day trips or, like this year, drive along the coast. It's a
good time to go, while the rates are still low, and before the tour-
ists take over. Charlie and the boys went fishing that weekend,
and the plan was, once he got back, we'd take Monday to get ourselves ready, then head out on Tuesday. Would have been a decent
plan, too, if Charlie hadn't thrown his back out.

"I still wanna go, Ida," he says.

"Charlie, you can hardly walk."

"Just give me a day or two; I'll pull it together."

What a mess! Hardly slept a wink that night what with him
tossing and turning around, stealing the covers. And the snoring? Unreal. Think: semi-truck with a cracked muffler.

Anyways, bad back or not, Charlie's up before me the next
morning, hobbling around the kitchen. I finally haul myself out
of bed, and go to pour myself a cup of coffee, when I notice
there's only two bananas in the fruit bowl.

Oh, no!

"Charlie, you eat a banana?"

"Half of one, yeah."

"I was saving those for banana bread!"

"Well, I needed some fruit for my cereal."

"I told you I was saving those for banana bread."

"Look, you still got two and a half."

He limps over to the fridge and gets out a Tupperware with the remains of the third banana.

"That's more like a quarter, Charlie. It's not enough! You need three bananas to make banana bread. I can't believe you did that!"

"Oh, come on!"

"It's one thing if you forgot I was going to make banana bread, but the fact that you remembered and did it anyway! I just don't get it! And what's so hard about closing this closet door?"

"It don't bother me if it's open."

"Well, it bothers me! I can't believe you ate that banana. God, the skin was almost entirely black!"

"Nah, it was fine inside."

"But why would you do that?"

"It was half a banana, Ida. Let it go!"

"It was three-quarters!"

I figured I better give myself a little time out because the ol' double-wide was feeling mighty close. I went outside and did some weeding (which is cheaper than therapy). Powered by my bad mood, I raced through the whole front bed before I ran out of steam.

From where I sit now, I know this argument was more about me feeling disappointed about our vacation than the banana bread. (Though I still can't believe Charlie did that. I mean, what was he thinking?) If I really wanted some homemade banana bread at that moment in time, I could've driven over to Bouchard's Farm Stand, where Alice makes a killer banana bread. I shouldn't have brought up the closet door at all. That's another issue and only serves to muddy the waters.

We call this muckraking and it's a big no-no when it comes to having a good, clean fight. Don't start bringing up crap from your past together or an ongoing resentment. Focus on the matter at hand. In the heat of the moment, did I really think Charlie was going to come around to my point of view about the closet door when we were really arguing about the bananas (which were much more important to me at that moment)? You know you're muckraking when you hear yourself saying things like, "Remember when . . ." or "You always . . ." or "You never . . ."

When you hear those words, take my advice: Just stop!

Recipes for Romance: I'm Sorry I've Been So Cranky Cookies

Whether you're cranky for a reason or not, the easiest person to take it out on is usually your mate. And the fastest way I know of snapping myself out of my snit, is to do something nice for someone. That someone is usually Charlie because, you know, he's there.

Making cookies of any sort is a good mood changer because you must concentrate on the task at hand—cracking the eggs, putting the ingredients together, beating the batter. It's all very therapeutic. Then, you get to methodically put spoonfuls of dough on a cookie sheet, while sneaking a little batter for yourself to keep up your strength. Even better, put on some fun music or watch a video while you're working away, and making cookies will put you right in no time.

If all that doesn't do the trick, hey, you still have fresh-from-the-oven cookies to eat. Take a plate of them into your craft room with some milk or tea or, heck, a glass of wine, and have yourself a nice little party. If your mood is really bad, bring in the heavy artillery—grab the ice cream.

Do You Want To Be Right Or Happy?

Love Story was wrong!

Love means never having to say you're sorry? What a crock of doo-doo! Love means *always* having to say you're sorry.

You'll have to do it less, though, if you stick to some basic rules. We hear a lot about good parenting, but what I'm talking about here is good partnering.

You know the drill: criticize the behavior, not the person. This works with a co-worker or when you're scolding yourself, too. "Leaving your coffee cup on the edge of the counter wasn't the brightest thing to do, Ida," sounds better than, "Ida, you're an idiot."

Use "I" instead of "you" when making your point. It sounds nicer and less nitpicky. For example, instead of saying, "You never replace the toilet paper roll when you use the last of it." You could say, "I feel uncared for when there's no toilet paper there when I need it." Just kidding! I know you're supposed to do this "I feel" thing, but here in Maine, I feel statements just don't come natural. But if it's something you can own, do it.

With this sort of thing, I'd wait until we were both in a good mood. Then my "I" statement would be something like, "Charlie, could you come in here a minute? The toilet paper roll is empty, and I just wanted to make sure you know where we keep replacement rolls." Said with a smile, of course.

Lastly, there's great power in saying, "I'm sorry." It doesn't mean you're saying your mate is right. It's a way of taking responsibly for your part of the fight. And sometimes, it's about forgiving yourself for saying or doing something you're not all that proud of. Saying "I'm sorry" is a gift. You give a gift without expecting anything in return. If you're saying it because you're hoping to guilt trip your husband into saying it back, you're going to end up even more miffed. And remember, it's never too late to say you're sorry. You may have to work up to it, cool off a little. But trust me, you'll feel better when you do. It comes down to this: do you want to be right or happy?

 ## Love Mahoosuc Mills Style: Go To Bed Mad

A few weeks ago, my niece Caitlin called and asked if she could come over because she needed my advice.

I could tell she was upset. "Sure, dear, come on over. I'll heat up some water for tea, and have my Certified Maine Life Guide Magic Moose Antlers at the ready!"

"Thanks, Aunt Ida." Poor Caitlin said this with a little hitch in her voice, like she was trying not to cry.

Charlie looks up from his paper. "What's up?"

"Oh, that was Caitlin. She's coming over in about an hour for some girl talk."

"Trouble in paradise?"

"That's what I'm guessing."

Charlie downs the rest of his coffee, and gets up from the kitchen table. "I'm gonna make myself scarce."

"Good thinking, but not so fast. I'm going to whip up a pan of brownies, and we could use some ice cream. Would you mind ...?"

"Not at all. I gotta head that way, anyhow."

That's my guy. He knows chocolate has a way of taking the edge off, and with any luck, there'll be some left over for him.

Caitlin and her boyfriend Adam are still living together. They left their winter rental with the outhouse, and are now up to the old Dugal Farm. They got chickens and a wonderful vegetable garden, and are even thinking about buying the place some day.

Caitlin arrives, and I could tell she'd been crying. "Oh, Caitlin, come here. Aunt Ida's gonna make it all better."

I wrap her in a big bear hug.

"But before we get into it," I said, "we need some nourishment. And I just happen to have some warm from the oven brownies right here."

> *I go to the freezer, and return with two pints of ice cream.*

I put the pan on the table, along with tea and a couple of bowls. I go to the freezer, and return with two pints of ice cream.

"The doctor is in!"

That got a chuckle out of her.

I says, "Take two of these and call me in the morning. Let's see, we have Coffee Heath Bar and Cherry Garcia."

We filled up our bowls and got down to business. Turns out Caitlin and Adam were arguing about something the night before. No need to get into the particulars. Suffice it to say, it was a big one.

Caitlin says, "You shouldn't go to bed mad, right? I mean, that's what they say. Even though we were both too tired, we kept going at it, and we ended up saying stuff we shouldn't have."

"Oh, Caitlin, believe me, I've been there, done that. I don't know who 'they' are, but sometimes I just want to ring their necks! I suppose, in a perfect world, that's a good rule. Trouble is, we don't live in a perfect world.

"Next time, if you're getting into it and you're beyond tired, stop talking and just go to bed. Same room, separate rooms, it don't matter. (Just don't leave the house. That's only gonna make matters worse.) Sleep on it. Things always look better in the morning. At the very least, you've calmed down and maybe you can actually hear what your mate is saying."

"Probably," she says, all teary-eyed. "Right now, I'm afraid the damage is done. I just feel so bad."

"I know, dear. But you and Adam love each other. You'll work it out."

"But he was up before me and left for work without saying good-bye."

"He's probably feeling as bad as you, Caitlin. Why don't you text him, say you're sorry?"

"I am sorry I said some of those things I did. But I still think I'm right."

"Well, he don't need to know what you're sorry about."

Just then, Caitlin's phone beeped. It was a text from Adam, saying he was sorry, and they'll talk when he gets home from work. And would she like him to pick up a pizza on the way? He's a keeper, that fella.

Well, that brightened Caitlin's mood right quick. We celebrated with even more brownies and ice cream. Then, I gave her some to take home to Adam. Not all of 'em, you understand because my Charlie's a keeper, too.

Rule of thumb: when you get to the point where you're just going around in circles, you're accomplishing nothing. Take a break from each other. Go for a ride or a walk or into your craft room or workshop. Go to bed, for God's sake! We give kids a time out. Why don't we do ourselves and our spouse the same courtesy?

And speaking of kids, my sister Reney wants to make sure I tell you that if you have kids, don't fight in front of them. I can't remember our parents ever having a big argument in front of us. I know they had disagreements, but they worked 'em out behind closed doors, when we couldn't overhear. It's real easy to say things you don't mean in the heat of the moment, and kids hear and remember everything. Don't put those precious little gems in the middle.

Straight Talk From the Barcalounger: When in Doubt, Hug it Out

Sometimes your wife's gonna be mad at you, and you'll have no idea why. Number one rule: don't ask her what's the matter. That'll only make her more irritated at you because you can't read her mind. Hey, it's not fair, but life ain't fair.

You have two approaches here. Get outta her way. That means finding something to do in your workshop or an errand to run or something. Believe me, when she's ready to talk about it, she'll find you. Or option two, hug her and tell her you love her. Sure, I know she's not being real loveable at that minute, but suck it up and do it anyway. Now Ida talked about this in the first book, and it took me years to realize it, but I can't stress this enough—do not stop hugging first. That'll only make matters worse. Just hang in there until she breaks the huddle.

Any luck, that hug and "I love you" will make things right as rain and you can skip the talking about it part all together. Worst case, she'll actually tell you what's bugging her.

No Sniping. Period.

Saturday night we went to the bean supper down to the Congo Church. If you've never been to one (and that would be a sad state of affairs), you usually sit family-style at big round tables. Well, at our table was a couple who'd obviously had an argument before the shindig, and had not left it in the car. All through dinner, they kept sniping at each other. Wow! Is that ever uncomfortable.

There's a big difference between sniping and some gentle ribbing. What is that difference, you might ask? Well, I'd say it's about whether you (the person doing it) are motivated by love or by wanting to make the other person feel miserable.

For instance, I have this thing about folks not taking down their Christmas decorations in a timely manner. Groundhog's Day—that's the official drop dead date.

So when Charlie and me are walking through the neighborhood with Scamp, I'll say, "I can't believe the Smiths still have their kissing ball up. It's past St. Patrick's Day, for God sake!"

> *I have this thing about folks not taking down their Christmas decorations in a timely manner. Groundhog's Day—that's the official drop dead date.*

And Charlie smiles and replies, "Would you like to leave a neighborly note?" This is an ongoing joke between the two us. Because honey, there are so many

people and things in this world that could benefit from my
micro-management, right?

But suppose Charlie said, "Why don't you put *that* on the
to do list you probably got going for them? Those curtain's
don't look closed perfect, either." Well, that feels a little mean,
doesn't it? Like it's referring to something he's miffed about.

Or, how about this: we're having dinner with another couple,
and someone says, "Are you supposed to trim back your rose
bushes in the spring or fall?" And Charlie goes, "Why don't you
ask Ida. I'm *sure she* has a rule about that." Icky, right? (I hate
even writing these examples, because it's not really in Charlie's
nature to act like that.)

No, a good relationship is about being kind and respectful.
That means instituting a sniping ban; in the house and in public. Throwing little zingers from the side lines is not showing
up with your whole self in your relationship. It's petty and
mean-spirited. This is why nipping resentments in the bud is so
important. Sniping usually has resentment at its core.

The sad thing is, I'm always gonna remember that couple for
how nasty they were that evening, and they'll never be on my
invite list when I throw a party. Do you want folks to remember you and your mate like that? I don't! It's simple, folks: what
happens in the double-wide, stays in the double-wide, and no
sniping allowed.

Make Up, Make Out

What's the best part about having a heated augment with your
spouse? Hot, "I'm so mad at you, I got to get it out in some
way" sex? Nah, that's more of a movie sort of thing, far as I can
remember.

To be honest, we haven't had a epic row in a dog's age. I think it's because we've pretty much worked through those big things. And frankly, as you get older, time has a way of smoothing the sharp edges off your personality. Basically, you stop trying to change the other person and start accepting them for who they are. Unless you've already cut your losses and moved on.

No, the best part about having a tiff is the makeup sex. Or maybe it's just a makeup cuddle, a batch of I'm-Sorry-I've-Been-So-Cranky cookies, and Charlie saying, "Let's go out to eat so you don't have to cook." Don't matter. It's the sweetness of closing the distance between you, of appreciating how lucky you are.

Getting Goin'

- If you feel the crankies coming on or resentment starting to build, head 'em off at the pass. Do something nice for your spouse. Ask for what you want. You know the drill.
- The next time your spouse asks you what you want to do this weekend or where you want to go to dinner, answer the question instead of asking him or her what they want.
- When you're both in a good mood, come up with a fair fight plan. Use this chapter as a starting point.
- The next time you're going 'round and 'round about something and getting nowhere, give yourself a time out.
- Once things settle down, take a moment to savor the coming together again.

Seven

How to Date Your Mate

All work and no play makes for a dull marriage. Think about it. Whether you use vegetable shortening or marshmallow fluff in your whoopie pie filling, it's the sweet stuff that holds it together. In a relationship, that sweet stuff is love, but it can get a little thin if you're not having fun together.

Thing is, the hustle and bustle of your everyday life can weigh you down. I know this personally. What with work, meal planning, keeping the house tidy and micro-managing Charlie, it's easy for me to get into a busy rut. And we don't even have kids! Day after day, it's the same thing. Before you know it, you're grunting at each other at breakfast and falling asleep in front of the tube in the evening. Weekends are filled with errands and chores around the house. Makes me tired just thinking about it.

It's not a lost cause, though. A little effort in this area can reap big rewards because fun is the secret ingredient that makes it all work. Could be as simple as laughing together at least once a day. If that means watching a stupid pet video on the internet, do it. It's what, three or four minutes of your time? And you don't even have to leave the house. Sitting shoulder to shoulder and laughing at YouTube videos of cats sitting like humans or dogs who've made a mess and know they've done wrong can perk you both up no end.

Ignite the Spark

Want to put a little spark back into your relationship? The easiest place to start is with yourself. Feeling good is contagious, and hopefully your spouse will get a contact high from all your hard work in this area. Then, they just might get inspired to raise their game. The worst thing that can happen is you'll have fun with your friends.

For example, a couple of Black Fridays ago, me and the Women Who Run With the Moose went shopping down to the Bangor Mall. We're browsing around Kohl's, and see that the shapewear is on sale.

To the uninitiated, shapewear or Spanx (Spankies, as we call 'em) are like old-fashioned girdles, only now they're made of Lycra or Spandex or some other space-age material probably developed by NASA. These miracles of modern engineering smooth everything out and hold it in.

So we decide to give the Shapewear a try. The holidays were coming up and we wanted to look our best. We grab a bunch in different shapes and sizes and take 'em into the dressing room. Oh, my God, did we ever laugh!

I started by trying on a Spanky/granny-panty-type thing. It came up to my waist, which, alas, is my problem area.

"Well," I says to the girls, "this is definitely not working."

"Ida," Betty says, while trying to stiffle a giggle. "I think you're gonna have to try one that goes up higher. Because, um, I'm lookin' at a certain degree of spillage."

"I know," I says, "major muffin top, huh?" I quickly graduated to an industrial strength Spanx that goes from the top of my knees, right up to my bra. It seemed to do the trick.

But the thing that really got us going was when Rita, who's tiny to begin with, tried on a Spanky slip in size small. Now, here's the deal: I don't care how slender you are (and if you're that thin, why are you bothering with a Spanky in the first place?) the thing with Spankies is, you gotta go with the large, or extra large or they're just too tight. But Rita didn't want to feel left out, so she disappears into the dressing room with that Spanky slip, and somehow managed to wedge herself into it.

Dot goes, "Come out here and model it for us, Rita."

"I can't," she squeaks.

"Why not?" says Celeste

"I . . . don't . . . think I can . . . walk!"

Then Shirley goes, "Bunny hop, Rita!"

And with that, Rita flings back the curtain and hops out, and the rest of us, half undressed and Spankied to the max, dissolve into fits of laughter. I mean, that silly kind where you can't get your breath. You start to talk, but you're laughing so hard you can't get the words out. Then, you get a stitch in your side.

"Stop! Stop!" Betty gasps. "My Spanky's so tight, it hurts when I laugh!"

And that got us going even more. Plus, we were starting to overheat from all that Spandex.

Then Rita, tears of laughter streaming down her face, goes, "I don't know . . . how . . . I'm going to get . . . this . . . thing off!"

I go, "We might need the Jaws of Life!"

> *And even though it wasn't her size, Shirley ended up having to buy the Spanky she had on. Why? Because she peed in it!*

With that, Shirley goes, "Uh oh . . . "

"What?" we all ask.

Shirley's face is all red, "I just peed my pants!"

"You mean, peed your Spanky!"

It took all five of us (five!) to pry Rita out of that slip. And even though it wasn't her size, Shirley ended up having to buy the Spanky she had on. Why? Because she peed in it!

Get it in Writing

"What are you making?" asks Charlie.

"An apple pie," I reply, "for tonight."

"What's goin' on tonight?"

"We're having dinner, remember? With Irene and Jimbo?"

"We are? When did this come up?"

"Couple of weeks ago. I told you!"

"News to me."

"No, it's not. Where's your calendar?"

Charlie pulls out his dog-eared pocket calendar.

"I know it's in there, Charlie. I remember watching you as you scribbled it in. Probably can't read your own handwriting."

Charlie fumbles through it. "Oh. Yeah. Guess I should look at it every now and then."

"Might be helpful. Anyhoo, if you want pie, we're having it at Irene and Jimbo's."

Folks, if you're planning on having fun together, get on the same page. That means putting it in your calendar, and—I shouldn't have to say this, but I will—checking your calendar every once and awhile. Whether you type it into your phone and share it on the cloud (whatever that means) or go old school like me (a pen and a big month-at-a-glance type deal), it's more likely to happen if you schedule it in. Putting it in writing will also help in the selective hearing department. Talk about it, write it down while he's watching and make him write it in his calendar (if he even uses one). Then, when the ol' spousal deafness kicks in, you can have yourselves a calendar show down. And voilà! There it is in black and white, baby!

Most of us have to pick our vacations from work in advance, so you don't have to worry about blocking those in. They're a given. But a good relationship takes a little more together time than that. I'm talking about going on a date once a week or maybe taking a long weekend together every quarter.

If you're the planner in the couple, this is your job. If you leave it to your mate, they might be just as happy sitting at home watching the tube. Nothing wrong with that, of course, but it can get a little same old, same old. There's nothing like getting outta the house together to keep the doldrums at bay.

I remember a dance a while back down to the Knights of Columbus when I was chatting with Shirley.

"Gee," I says, "look at the boys over there all happy, laughing. Probably telling dirty jokes."

"No doubt," Shirley agrees.

"Nice to see 'em having fun, though."

"Now he's all jolly, but getting Junior here was another story. You'd think he was going to his own execution."

"He didn't want to come?"

"Oh, he'd had a hard week at work. Totally forgot about the dance. Grumble, grumble, groan. You know the drill."

"Sure do."

"So I says to him, 'Junior, I know it would be easier to just stay home, doing nothing. But we're going to that dance and having fun whether we want to or not.' I figured it'd do him good, blow off a little steam, put the week behind him. Now look at him over there, yucking it up."

"Sometimes, Shirley, they just need a loving push out the door."

"I was thinking more like a swift kick in the pants!"

Put Your Money Where Your Mouth Is

Sometimes, investing a little money up front will help you really commit to your together time. Buy a season ticket or pass to a sporting event, theater or concert series. Scout out deals on things you wouldn't normally try. Once you buy it, you have to use it, right? You could invest in a hobby like golf, kayaking, or snowshoeing. Once you have the gear, it's a pretty cheap date. Well, golf will run you a little more than the other two, but remember what Betty said—for her and Pat, golf's the key to a happy marriage.

In the wicked good deal department, if you're 62 or older, for ten dollars you can buy a National Parks and Federal Recreational Lands Senior Pass. This is good for your lifetime, and allows you to take your vehicle and up to three other people into the park or protected land for free. You also get discounts on other things like camping and launching your boat.

Dates don't just have to be at night. Gas up the car and take a road trip for an afternoon, the whole day, or a weekend. Visit a maple sugar shack in spring. How about apple picking in fall? Go for a walk by the ocean or to a museum. None of this stuff has to break the bank, either, because you can pack your lunch and eat at a rest area or scenic overlook. Plus, great conversations happen when you're in the car, just the two of you, without any distractions. Men seem to be more comfortable talking when they're shoulder to shoulder instead of facing each other head-on. Check it out next time you're at a party or something. Watch how men stand when they talk to each other, and you'll see.

Try being a tourist in your town, city, state, or country. Ask yourself, if someone was visiting from away, where would I take 'em? What would I show 'em? Charlie and me spent our honeymoon on the coast of Maine, but didn't really see much of anything except the inside of our motel room. Since then, we've had a great time exploring the coast.

Just Like Riding a Bike

You could also try rediscovering something you loved as a kid, though that can be dicey because as you get older, things are not always as you remember them. That was the topic of conversation last week when the Women Who Run With the Moose got together for our regular girls night out. Rita was hosting, and she was serving these watermelon margaritas, which, to be honest, are kind of an acquired taste. Luckily, after half a glass, you don't really care! Plus, they're garnished with melon balls, so they qualify as a serving of fruit, right?

Dot says, "Remember how I told you that Tommy and me were thinking about buying a couple of bikes? You know, it was something we used to do as teenagers, ride around together. We thought it'd be fun."

"Oh, no," goes Shirley.

"That sounds like it's destined to end in tears," I chime in.

"You're not far from the mark, Ida. First thing to start crying was our bank account. When did bikes get to be so expensive?"

111

"Geez," Rita says, "why didn't you just buy a couple at a yard sale or something?"

"You know Tommy and his toys. He figured if we're going to do it, we might as well do it right. Bikes sure have come a long way since our old one speeds. Plus, now you got all the paraphernalia to go with it: water bottle, helmet, gloves . . . "

"You didn't get a pair of them biking shorts did you?" Rita says. "After a certain age, bike shorts and a helmet aren't all that attractive."

"No, we drew the line at the bike shorts. The helmets were off-putting enough what with the tell-tale helmet hair. Worse than hat hair, I can assure you."

"Okay, okay, we're dying to know. How'd you make out with the bikes?" I ask.

> *It's just me with this dorky helmet on, riding the brake so I don't pick up too much speed, fall off and break a hip.*

"Well, we get the things home, and Tommy rides to the end of the street and back. Then he looks at me and goes, 'Not like I remember it.' And he was right! Not even close. First off, you got all them gears to figure out."

"And the wind's not whipping through your hair because of the helmet."

"Right!"

Rita jumps in, "Oh, I loved that. Racing down the hill, feeling free."

"There's none of that," Dottie says. "It's just me with this dorky helmet on, riding the brake so I don't pick up too much speed, fall off and break a hip."

"Oh, honey!"

"I don't know what we were thinking. That we'd recapture our youth or something? And we spent all that money on bikes . . . "

"Hang in there, Dot," Betty says. "It's got to get better. You know, practice?"

"I'm trying. In fact, a couple of days ago, I went out for a ride before work, trying to get more comfortable with it, so's I can keep up with Tommy. When I got home, I sent him a text. I have it right here: 'went biking. did good except I fell at the end but I'm alright.' He sends me this one back: 'happy to hear you broke bones.' I think he might have left some words out."

"Sounds that way."

"What happened to just jumping on your bike and riding fast and carefree?"

"At our age, there's a lot of things that aren't as good as you remember," says Celeste.

"Like sex," Shirley jumps in. "It's serviceable. Sometimes, I have to admit, it's pretty good. But it doesn't quite, I don't know, pack the punch I remember."

We shake our heads in agreement and sigh.

"Well, one thing that never changes," I says, "is the importance of fruit in your diet. Another round of watermelon margaritas, everyone?"

 ## Recipes For Romance: Destination Eats

Some food is just worth the drive. One of our favorite road trip dates in going to Red's Eats in Wiscasset for their lobster rolls. Oh, baby, plumb chucka full of fresh lobster meat and served on a buttery roll! And they put the mayo and butter on the side, so you can dress it up the way you like. Plus, they serve ice cream!

A great Sunday day trip is to head to the A1 Diner in Gardiner. Charlie and me love diners to begin with, and they have a great menu. But Sundays at the A1 are special. Their menu of knock-your-socks-off choices have a creative twist that will make your taste buds sit up and take notice.

Down south in Maine, you gotta stop at Flo's Hot Dogs in Cape Neddick. It's been owned by the same family since forever. Order the house special with their own relish, mayo, and a little celery salt. Warning: God help you if you're over fifteen and ask for catsup.

And while you're in the area, there's Congdon's Donuts in Wells serving one of the best donuts in Maine, maybe the world. Babe's donuts down to the Busy Bee are pretty darn good, too, but Congdon's are pure heaven.

What's your destination food road trip? Diners? BBQ? Poutine? Homemade ice cream? Do a little research, gas up the car and go. Happy eating!

Staycation Do's and Don'ts

Up until the economy tanked, staycation wasn't even a word. There's a reason for that. See how only half the word resembles vacation? That's a hint as to the outcome of most staycations. At best, they're kind of like a vacation. At worse, they're more like a week spent in the Gulag.

Charlie and me learned this the hard way. We'd never taken a staycation, so we thought we'd give it a try. We even made a plan. We'd scrape and repaint the deck the first weekend, because it needed it wicked bad. Then we'd spend the rest of the week doing little day trips, you know, making it up as we went along.

Trouble is, once we started the deck project, it just wouldn't end. Because that's what house projects do, right? They take at least two or three times longer than you think they're gonna. Why do we have to keep relearning this?

We must have scraped for two days straight. We're already starting to snap at each other. Then we put a coat of paint on. That took forever. But, since we gotta wait for it to dry between coats, why not clean out the shed? And heck, why not mulch the yard, while we're at it? Maybe wash the windows, inside and out. That sounds like fun. It never ends. It. Never. Friggin. Ends!

That's a hint as to the outcome of most staycations. At best, they're kind of like a vacation. At worse, they're more like a week spent in the Gulag.

Oh, our friends were wicked impressed. "You two got so much done together!"

"Yeah, well, don't think for a minute that it had anything remotely to do with taking time off from work."

I did put my foot down about cooking suppers. In my opinion, if I have to plan and cook dinner, it's not a vacation. That's why I'm not big on renting a condo or camp or something. That always ends up with me cooking supper like I do most every night of the year, only with a better view.

On our staycation, the last thing I felt like doing after a "relaxing" day of manual labor, was getting all dolled up and driving to Bangor for dinner and a movie. So, I had Charlie pick up a couple of Italian sandwiches one night, meatball subs the next, a pizza and a pint or two of ice cream (since he was out anyways). And we'd watch a movie on the tube until falling asleep on the couch.

We did take a couple of day trips, but frankly, it was a relief to go back to work, just so we could rest up!

Don't let this happen to you! If you're thinking about a staycation, plan it like you would your vacation. First off, no house chores, period. That's because you're on vacation, remember?

Come up with some things you'd like to do and schedule 'em in. Don't want it so set in stone? Longing for more spontaneity? Take your list of things, write 'em on pieces of paper and put 'em into a small bucket, a jar, a basket, whatever. It could be just the name of a nearby place you'd like to explore or a restaurant you'd like to try. Every morning of your staycation, draw one outta the basket (or more, if they're small), and do it.

This sort of thing also works great for your weekly date, or long weekend getaways. Have an ongoing "fun jar" or "date basket," and if at any time you hear or think of something fun you'd like to try, write it on a piece of paper and put it in. (No chores allowed.) Can't think of anything to do with your spouse this week? Bored with the same old, same old? Just pick something from the bucket o' fun.

Don't Waste Your Time

The biggest thing to remember when trying new things with your spouse is to really commit. If you're gonna do something in a half-hearted way, it's a waste of time. You know what I'm talking about. You're going through the paces in a "I'm doing this for you and you're going to owe me big time" sort of way. Frankly, that's not a very attractive attitude. I know I keep saying this, but it all comes down to showing up with your whole self and being responsible for your own personal happiness.

That said, there are some things that you know are going to be a stretch for your spouse, and would be more fun to do with your friends or by yourself. Don't ask him or her to slog through it just because you've agreed to try different things together. This is about doing things to enhance your relationship, not testing the love and commitment of your spouse. Play nice, people!

My rule of thumb is this: If Charlie's wicked excited about doing something, and I'm iffy, I'll usually go along with it. The way I look at it, he's excited enough for both of us, and seeing him happy makes me happy. Plus, the destination is only part of the date, right? We have a scenic drive, and the easy chatting that happens in the car. I'll research a good restaurant to eat at on the way. Maybe stop for ice cream on the way home, or visit a junktique store or two.

Whether you decide that something is going to be wicked fun or a total drag, most likely, you're gonna be right. I choose fun every time. Negotiate. Build a two-part date with something you're excited about and something your spouse wants to do. Bring a good book to read, so if he's at a museum taking forever looking at that exhibit of hot rods and muscle cars, you can go outside, sit in the sun and read. He's not worried about you being bored, and you're happy with a little down time. And remember to always bring a snack so you don't get cranky.

Grillin' Like a Man

One Saturday last spring, Charlie suggested that for our date, we go shopping for a new gas grill. The old one was plumb worn out, so it was time. I thought this sounded more like a *chore* than a *date*, but he was excited about it. And I figured there'd be stuff there to hold my attention. Besides, how long could it take, right?

Well, it takes about three hours, apparently. Charlie's not an impulse buyer. No, he's what you might call a comparison shopper, debating the merits of this one or that one, different "features," and asking questions, questions, and more questions. Honest to God! Like the gas grill is some kind of fancy sports

car. And of course, there's a whole bunch of other guys there
doing the same thing.

The fact is grilling, for the most part, is a man's territory.
Don't get me wrong, I use the gas grill. But when I do, it's
called cooking supper. When Charlie grills, it's a national holiday. And there's beer involved. And usually a gang of other guys
standing around, staring at the fire, trading tips on cooking
meat, and talking about their gas grills. You know, the "my grill
is bigger than your grill" sort of a thing.

The manufacturers know this, and, boy, they don't disappoint.
I tell you, there were some big, honkin' gas grills at the store.
Like, Hindenburg-big. Sleek black or shiny, chrome deals, with
guys checking out all the bells and whistles, kicking the tires,
and (swear to God, I actually saw this) caressing the darn things.
In fact, I found myself getting kinda jealous of one grill (going
for close to $4,000 buck-a-roonies) when I saw the way Charlie
was lusting after it.

"Check this out, Ida," he says, eyes all agog. "Two side burners."

"I can see that, but I think I'm good with the burners inside."

"Yeah, but did you hear that fella? He says we can use it to
cook lobster without stinking up the house."

"Charlie, how often do we have lobsters? Once a year? Besides,
when was the last time you cooked something on a burner?"

"Well, you'd be in charge of the burner."

"Sweetheart," I says, exiting the grilling department, "there
ain't a gas grill big enough to accommodate both of us cooking
at the same time."

I killed more time browsing around in the home decorating
section, looking at all them shiny new kitchens and bathrooms.
Checking out the lights and area rugs. Oh, and I picked up a
few annuals and a hanging plant from the garden center. Every

once in a while checking back with Charlie, to make sure he wasn't getting carried away.

As wacky as the gas grill thing is, it's better than the charcoal grills of old. Holy guacamole! This is before people were using all natural charcoal and mesquite and what not and lighting them with those funnel gizmos. No, I'm talking a friggin' mountain of charcoal briquettes, the aforementioned knuckleheads drinking beer, squirting lighter fluid, and playing with matches. Duck and cover!

Well, we finally settled on a gas grill somewhere between kiddy size, as Charlie called it, and ginormous. And yes, it has enough gauges and gadgets to preserve Charlie's manhood without breaking the bank.

So it's afternoon by the time we make it to the checkout, right? I'm hungry as all get out (I forgot snacks, can you believe it?). As Charlie and me are standing in line with the grill, a grill cover, and some new grilling tools, he turns to me all perky and says, "So how come you're getting another hanging plant? I thought we already had one."

Yes, you heard that right.

I stared back at him hard. I pictured myself doing something with Charlie's new grilling tongs that I can't mention here.

Catching on, Charlie goes, "It sure is a pretty color, though. Say, how about we head over to Ruby Tuesdays after this? I know how much you like their salad bar, dear."

 ## Straight Talk From the Barcalounger: Plan B

How long has it been since you took your wife on a date? Can't remember? Then it's about time.

Quit complaining, it's not rocket science. Heck, we dated as kids. Sure, we were eager to please and had a little more energy back then. We were more than willing to put in some effort, hoping to reap the benefits, if you know what I'm saying. It's the same now, guys. Just getting by ain't enough. You can't do that and expect to still be happily married when they roll you into Mahoosuc Green Senior Living.

Trust me, dating is tricky business, and it can go south real quick. You won't even know what went wrong. But be warned, always have a Plan B. Mine is to ask Ida if she wants to go get lunch or ice cream or check out the candy shop. Yeah, I'm not hungry, but it don't matter. When she gets that look in her eye, I don't even try to figure out what I did or didn't do, I move straight to something in the food category to save the date.

When the going gets tough, chocolate and a big hug can usually get things back on an even keel faster than playing twenty questions. Try Plan B.

Recipe for Romance: Fish or Cut Bait

In Mahoosuc Mills, one of the best testimonials for investing in your relationship comes from Chuck and Roberta (Bobbie) Robbins. I know this firsthand because you know how we all like to confide in our hairdresser or bartender? As a cashier down to the A&P, folks tend to confide in me, too, even if they don't always know they're doin' it. Checking out a person's groceries is more intimate than you imagine. Like you find out who is drinking a little too much, who has a Doritos habit, who is addicted to the *National Enquirer,* and who buys a lot of unmentionables. You see the same folks once a week, minimum, so you get a sense whether they're feeling their oats or not.

One day I'm working register three, per usual, cashing out Bobbie, making conversation, like you do. "How's that cute little dog of yours? Blah, blah. And the kids? Your youngest getting ready for college? I can't believe it. Blah, blah. And your wonderful husband? How's Chuck doing?"

"Good," Bobbie replies, "I guess."

The way she said "I guess" didn't sound so good.

"He's traveling so much with his job, it's like we're two ships passing in the night."

Hmmm. Another red flag.

So, time passes, and Bobbie and Chuck's youngest heads off to college. Bobbie's now buying fewer groceries, as you'd expect. But then, one day, I see Chuck in the store. That kind of brought me up short. Chuck never comes into the A&P—too busy. He went through the express lane, so I couldn't chat him up. But the next time I see Bobbie in line, I pounce. "Chuck was in last week. Didn't get a chance to say hi. How's he doing?"

Bobbie looks out at the parking lot. "I wouldn't know, Ida," she sighs. "We, uh, separated a few weeks ago."

"Oh, I'm so sorry to hear that, Bobbie. How you holding up, dear?"

"As good as can be expected, I guess. It wasn't any big dramatic thing, Ida. What with the kids and Chuck's job, we just kind of drifted apart, I guess."

Hard to know what to say to that. "Oh, Bobbie, my heart goes out to you." That's the best I could come up with.

Another six or seven months pass and I see Chuck and Bobbie down to the A&P, shopping separately. Neither of 'em looked too happy, but Bobbie at least, seemed to be making an effort.

"Bobbie, don't you look nice," I said. "I love that shade of lipstick on you."

"Thanks, Ida. I got talked into going to one of them speed dating things in Bangor tonight, if you can believe it."

"Good for you! You'll have to tell me how you make out."

"I'm wicked nervous, but what do I have to lose? Wish me luck."

"You don't need it. You look fabulous!"

The next time I see her, Bobbie's a little less perky. "How was the speed dating?" I ask.

"Grueling! The only good thing was that you didn't have to spend a lot of time with each guy. What an odd assortment of geezers and geeks. Wasn't a total loss, though. I had a drink with a couple of the other gals after, and we really hit it off. Going to a dance together next week." Bobbie sighs.

More time passes, and one day I see Bobbie and Chuck in the A&P shopping together, gigglin' in the wine aisle. I'm too busy to do more than wave as they stroll out arm in arm, all atwitter.

The next time Bobbie's into the A&P, she comes to my register to cash out, looking happy as pie.

"Bobbie," I say, "I don't have to ask how you're doing. I can see it on your face."

"Yup, Ida, Chuck and me are back together."

"Well, I saw the two of you two last week, looking like a couple of love birds."

"It's like we're teenagers again, Ida."

"What happened?"

"Well, we started out just talking on the phone. You know, coordinating things for when the kids come home. Then, sometimes, Chuck would call, and we'd just talk on and on about nothing in particular. We'd meet down to the Busy Bee every now and then for breakfast. And then hey, I'm going to Bangor to see a movie, you want to come? Before we knew it, it's like we were dating again. And it was good. Heck, it was great. We started really talking to each other like we hadn't in years. Sometimes, he'd sleep over."

"Good for you!"

"I know! So one thing led to another, and we agreed that at our age, sure, we could potentially meet someone else and still have a good twenty, twenty-five years with 'em. But that would be a gamble. We might not find the right person. But if we put some of that same time, energy, and money into our relationship, we might end up with something really wonderful. It was great once, why not again?"

"Plus, you have the kids, and all that shared history."

"Right. The kids are over the moon about it."

"I'll bet!"

"Chuck's still away a lot on business, but we're working on that. I go with him every now and then. And he's trying to hammer out a deal where he can step down to about half as many trips. The big difference is, when he's home, he's home. He's not in the den catching up on work or doing deals into the night. And we talk and text a lot when he's away. It's not perfect, but it's so much better than it was."

"Sounds great."

"Plus, now that the kids are gone, I'm getting more used to having the house to myself. When me and Chuck were separated, I signed up for an art class down to the Community Center, and I'm still doing that. I realized I used to love painting and doing artsy stuff. I'd totally lost track of it."

"Good for you, Bobbie! You're an inspiration!"

Bobbie puts her hand on mine. "Thanks, Ida, for your support. The whole separation thing was hard, wicked hard. But if that's what it took to get to us where we are now, it was worth every minute!"

Getting Goin'

- Do one thing (at least) to spiff yourself up.
- Sit down with your mate, calendars in hand, and schedule date time once a week for the next month.
- While you're at it, put a weekend getaway in your calendar, too.
- Put your money where your mouth is. Buy a season pass to a sporting event, theater or outdoor festival. Can't afford that? Look at the schedule of upcoming games, shows or concerts, and buy tickets to one thing. You're more likely to do it if you commit ahead of time.
- Is there a sport or hobby you'd like to try together? Kayaking? Fishing? Snowshoeing? Golfing? Biking? Take a lesson or rent equipment for a day and see if you like it.
- Create a Fun Jar and fill it with date ideas. Each of you start with five options. Think of new ideas as you go along.
- If money's tight, start a Free Fun Jar. Fill it with fun stuff that don't cost anything. There are no excuses as to why you can't have fun together.
- Negotiate a two-part date with your mate: something for them, something for you.
- Try doing something your spouse really wants to do, but you're iffy about. Do it with a good attitude.
- What's your Plan B? How can you prepare in case you have to use it?

Eight

Uh, oh! What To Do When the "You Know What" Hits the Fan

So far I've mainly talked about dealing with things in your marriage that you can actually control, mainly you and your attitude. But real life happens, and into every marriage a little doo-doo must fall. What then?

Basically, the same rule applies. You can't control the world (though that hasn't stopped me from trying!), but you can control your attitude. That doesn't mean ignore the situation, but accept where you're at and do the best you can with what you've got. Acceptance is key. You can't move forward if you're fighting where you're at.

Working with your partner will make things easier, but to be a good team player, you must show up with your whole self. Sure, there will be times when one of you is down in the dumps and the other will lend a hand and vice versa. That's called a marriage. But it's the vice versa in that sentence that's most important. It's critical to be there for each other in good times and not so good times.

Not Everyone Can Play Quarterback

Let's talk about teamwork. Not everyone can play quarterback, right? In fact, not everyone *wants* to play quarterback. A championship team is the one where folks play the position that suits 'em. If you work with that, solving problems gets a whole lot easier.

If you're married to the world's nicest guy, asking him to march in and tell off the car repair guy—because after $900 your car's still not running right—isn't going to work. You just have to realize that being the squeaky wheel is your job. Maybe you wish it wasn't, but think about it: If he always got worked up and gave folks a hard time, he wouldn't be the guy you married, would he?

Being a team player means rolling up your sleeves and doing what needs to be done without having to be asked (cleaning out the vegetable bin, packing your share of boxes or going to get milk when you see there's not enough left for your wife's morning coffee). Sometimes being a team player means taking care of yourself (asking for help instead of waiting until things are outta control), or taking care of him (making the house a cozy place by cooking his favorite meal when work is particularly stressful). And, let's face it, sometimes you're the teammate who just sits back and listens or doles out some tough love by saying the things no one else dares to say.

By the way, worrying is *not* a legitate job on this playing field. Some folks mistake worrying with *actually doing* something. Wrong! You can worry on your own time, the middle of the night, say (although I wouldn't recommend it), but you don't get to worry as your only contribution to a difficult situation. It's just not fair to your mate!

Is That an Air Freshener in Your Pocket?

Have you ever gotten a phone call like this one?

"Hey, there Dad. How you doing?"

"Not so good. I fell and hurt my knee wicked bad."

There are no shortage of things that can stress you out. The unexpected, like that phone call, your car breaking down, or a blizzard ruining your plans. But the biggies are: money, children, work, and the Red Sox, not necessarily in that order. As you get older though, the sources of stress shift with more emphasis on your aging parents and health—theirs and yours.

Nowadays when we get together with friends, Charlie and me can't help but notice that the conversation has changed. We used to talk about everyone's kids. Now we swap stories about our elderly parents.

Charlie's parents, Simone and André, have both passed away. Been gone, oh, twenty years now, and I still miss 'em. Especially Simone. What a character!

My favorite Simone story happened one Christmas a few years before she died. Charlie's cousin Ralph sent her a crocheted toilet-paper cover for Christmas, complete with the roll inside. It was the kind without the doll on top. So a few weeks after Christmas, I'm visiting with Simone, and I ask her, "Simone, where's that cute little crocheted toilet-paper cover that Ralph gave you? I didn't see it in the bathroom."

"Oh my God," she says, her face turning beet red. "A toilet-paper cover! I wondered why Ralph sent me a hat and only gave

André a roll of toilet paper. I wore the hat to Mass last Sunday. It was so tight, it gave me a headache!"

Anyhoo, my Mom passed twelve years ago, but I still find myself walking to the phone to call her and ask her advice or to share a funny story. Mom was sick for almost five years, and Charlie was there for me, ready with a hug or a shoulder to cry on.

Thankfully, Dad's still with us. He lives over to Mahoosuc Green, our senior living facility in town. He bought in a couple years after mother passed away. Their old house was just too big and lonely. You should've seen him after he first moved in. He looked about ten years younger than when Mom was failing because he no longer had to worry about her suffering and maintaining the house. Once he settled into Mahoosuc Green, Dad was like the Energizer Bunny, always off bowling or golfing or what not. He barely had time to get a hair cut. And weren't those widows just buzzin' around him like flies to honey. Actually, they still are. He's a good catch: nice looking man, good head of hair. And, he still drives at night.

"Dad," I says, "you're in a seller's market. You play your cards right, you could have a different casserole every night of the week, if you know what I'm saying!"

Dad's been at Mahoosuc Green for ten years now. He just turned eighty-three, but, frankly the wheels are starting to come off. He fell last October and pulled a ligament in his arm. Didn't tell my sister Irene or me about it for days.

When he finally did I asked, "Did you call the doctor, Dad?"

"No, it was a Sunday. I didn't want to bother him."

Sigh.

"I have my regular appointment scheduled a week from Monday." Honest to God!

Few days later, we're having lunch, and I'm watching him use both hands to lift his cup of coffee. "Gee, Dad, are you okay to drive with your arm like that?"

"Oh, sure," he says. "I gotta use two hands to get the key in the ignition, but once I do, I'm good to go."

Dad didn't bounce back the way he used to, but he could still drive, bowl and attend the weekly dance down to the Elks. He went to physical therapy, and I guess he was pretty good about doing his exercises.

But this latest fall was a major set back. Man, if it wasn't for one of them widows, Constance Hughey, who knows how long he would have gone without telling Irene and me. Connie says to him, "Either you call the girls or I'm gonna." So he did. Secretly, I think he kinda likes women bossing him around. It's a good thing, too.

"Dad," Irene says, "you're under new management."

I chime in, "The good news is the new management looks a lot like the old."

Irene and me both took the next day off from work, and we laid down the law. We made him agree to go to the doctor. We managed to wrangle a last minute appointment with "the kid," as my Dad calls him, although the doctor's my age. Dad didn't break nothing, thank God, but he sprained his right knee something fierce. The kid told him to ice it and take ibuprophen. Maybe get a walker. And no driving, period.

"Are you tellin' me I'm under house arrest?" Dad asks.

"Yes, I am," the kid replies.

We stopped at the Rite Aid on the way home. The walker was a hard sell, but Dad did agree to get a cane.

"Dad, we'll be back in a minute," I says. "You need anything else while we're in there? You got an ice pack, right?"

"No. Why don't you pick me up one of those."

Irene and me fast walk into the Rite Aid, shaking our heads.

Irene goes, "You mean to tell me doesn't have an ice pack?"

"Unbelievable! When he hurt his arm you can bet the physical therapist told him to go home and ice it."

"No wonder his arm wasn't getting any better!"

"We need some chocolate."

"Yes, we do. But first, weapons at the ready!"

And with that we both whip out our lipsticks and reapply. Because, you know, fresh lipstick always makes you feel better.

Then, we move into high gear—ice pack, chocolate, cane, chocolate, ibuprofen, did I mention chocolate? Back at the ranch, we arrange to have Dad's meals brought to him, for one of us to check in on him every day, see if he needs anything.

Later that week, we notice Dad's stopped shaving, and we suspect he's not showering.

"Dad," I say, "when was the last time you took a shower?"

"Day I fell."

"That was almost week ago. Why aren't you showering?"

"Afraid I'll fall again."

"Geez Louise! Why didn't you say something? We'll get a nurses aid to come in and help you."

"Oh, I don't need that. I'll just put an air fresher in my pocket."

"Dad, a shower will make you feel so much better. You know what Mom used to say: 'Look good, smell good, feel good.'"

The Talk

Is it time for "the talk"? No, not the sex talk with your kids. I mean talking to your parents about, you know, all the things you don't want to talk to 'em about and they don't want to think of—death. Before and after.

The best time for the talk is before it's an emergency. It is hard to make good decisions when everyone's stressed out or your parent can't communicate with you because they're unconscious or suffering from dementia. It's especially important to have everything organized if you live in a different town or state than your parents. I think it helps to stop thinking in terms of end of life. It's really all about quality of life, and who doesn't want that for their loved ones?

Thankfully, Irene works down to the senior center in town, so she deals with this kind of thing all the time. She has great suggestions for going about this which I'll be sharing here and in Chapter 9. You may have to spend a little time and money up front, but trust me, doing it right will save you time, money, and a lot of worry in the end, and that, my friends, is good for your relationship.

First off, there's a great website called *The Conversation Project* (theconversationproject.org) that even has a starter kit you can download. It takes you through having that talk with your loved one step by step. Check it out.

Is there a senior center in the town where your parents live? If so, see what they have to offer. They may have some fun classes for your Mom, senior daycare to spell your Dad from taking care of your Mom, or volunteers who can help get your loved one to the doctors or grocery shopping. How about an Agency on Aging in your area? They tend to have Meals on Wheels and other great resources.

If your parent is still at home and you're worried about them falling, there's the Lifeline. For the uninitiated, that's the thingy your senior wears on their wrist or around their neck, so if they fall, they just have to press a button and help is on the way. A lot of time, it's not the fall that causes lasting damage, it's laying undiscovered for hours without medical care.

If they won't wear a Lifeline, call the local police. Some of them have a program that requires your senior to call the station by a certain time each day or the police will check on 'em. This is typically a free service.

Make a Go Kit with everything you'll need if you get an emergency call. It should have a list of their medications and doctors, medical proxy, and power of attorney in it. While you're at it, put that medication list, doctors, and your contact numbers in an envelope and stick it on their fridge, clearly marked for the EMTs, just in case.

Knowing that your parents have their ducks in a row medically and financially reduces stress and that's good for your marriage. And once it's taken care of, keeping information current is easy.

There are also folks who specialize in working with seniors like geriatric care managers and elder law attorneys. "The wonderful thing about these people," Irene says, "is that they love working with older folks and are super good at it."

Geriatric care managers can really help if you live far away. They can take care of the day to day with your folks and be your eyes and ears on the ground. Don't need that much care? You can consult with a geriatric care manager, with or without your parent, and they'll help you create a long and short-term plan. They know the in's and out's of the system, which is amazingly helpful. All that bureaucracy can be hard to manage without the inside scoop. Plus, having someone else guide the conversation and ask the hard questions is worth the dough, believe me.

Same thing goes with an elder law attorney. They know how to set things up so the money's there when your parent needs it. They'll help you get paperwork in order and advise you what to look for in a facility, whether it's independent or assisted living. (Tip: always eat lunch in the dining room of the place you're considering and talk with the residents.) If you're worried about dementia in your loved one, it's good for the attorney to meet the family when all is well, so they'll know that you're on the same page as their memeory starts to slip. You might already have a lawyer, but an elder law attorneys is trained in this area. As my Dad says, "You don't go to a plumber to redo your fuse box."

Lifeline, Purple Cantaloupes and Other Senior Moments

Celeste, Rita, Betty, Dot, Shirley, and me got together for our girls night out a few weeks ago. Betty was hosting and she whipped up a batch of her Marvelous Marcel Bars. Oh, man, oh, man: to die for! I mean, what's not to like about something made with not only an entire bag of chocolate chips, but a bag of peanut butter chips, too?

After wolfing down one with a white wine chaser, Shirley goes, "Thanks, Betty. I needed that."

"Tough day?" I ask.

"Not one of Mini's better ones."

Mini is Shirley's mom. Everyone calls her Mini because she's over six feet tall. She lives in the mother-in-law apartment Junior built onto their house. Shirley's one of five and the only girl, so you know what that means: caretaking always falls to the daughter.

Betty asks, "Did she leave the stove on again?"

"Nope, we disconnected it. Thinking of getting her an easy bake oven."

"Poor dear," Rita adds. "What a good cook she was. I still remember her butterscotch cream pie."

"Me, too! That homemade butterscotch was a slice of heaven, huh?"

"Nothing like it!"

"How long has she been living with you now, Shirley?" I ask.

"Two years. That's the kicker. Just when I'm thinkin' she's all settled in, she'll have a day like this where she keeps asking to go home. Over and over. Can you pass me another one of them chocolate peanut butter thingies? What do you call 'em?"

"Marvelous Marcel Bars."

"That they are. Thanks, dear. Anyways, twice this morning, I put her in the car, drove 'round the block and then announced we were home. That usually works."

"It's all new, all the time," Celeste says.

"Not today. She still wouldn't settle down."

"What'd you do?" Dot asked.

"Well, I asked her to find me a purple cantaloupe in the fridge. That kept her busy for a while. Then, just like that, she was fine."

"You're a good daughter, Shirley!" I says.

"Peeshaw, enough about me. What's up with the rest of you?"

"I got a funny one," Betty says, "along the same lines. Happened to my Dad, day before yesterday. You know he's got that Lifeline, right?"

Rita goes, "My Mom's having none of it. How'd you ever talk him into getting one?"

"Well, with Lifeline, it's a two talk deal. First, you have talk them into getting one. Then you have to talk them into actually wearing the darn thing!"

"Ain't that the truth."

"Well, Dad got the Lifeline. Fine, but he wasn't wearing it, and I was stressed about him all alone in that big house. I kept complaining to Pat about it. Finally, Pat says to me, 'Look, you're going about it all wrong. Don't ask him to do it for himself; ask him to do it for you, you know, to put your mind at ease.'"

"Brilliant!" says Rita. "I wonder if that works with husbands, too. You know, about getting him to do stuff."

Celeste goes, "With your husband, it's easier to make him think it's his idea." We all agree.

"So I talked with Dad, again," Betty continues, "and I'll be darned, it worked! He's pretty good about wearing it now. That's what he tells me anyways. He's got the one that goes around your neck. Now, you know my Dad's a good sleeper. He can doze off morning, noon or night even after two cups of high test coffee."

"God," says, Dot. "I wish I could sleep like that."

"Doesn't even hear the cell phone clipped to his belt, even if it's set on stun! Anyhoo, he's kicked back in his recliner, watching the tube (napping, really) when all of sudden, there's this commotion. He wakes up to find the EMT's with a stretcher right there in his den."

"What? Did he set the Lifeline off by mistake or something?"

"I guess."

"Bet that woke him up right quick," I say.

"Don't know who was more surprised, Dad or the EMTs."

"Classic," Dot muses. "It's always something, isn't it?"

"How about getting them to admit they need hearing aids?"

"That's another two talk deal. Getting them, then getting them to wear 'em."

"Or how about using their cane?"

"I've given up on that one. Mom's just too proud. 'Makes me look old,' she says."

"It helps to go to their doctors appointments with them," I chime in. "That way you can ask the question, like about the cane, and someone else gets to be the bad guy."

"Right!"

"I keep trying to get Tommy to go with his parents," Dot adds, "but they're so private, you know? It's a hard sell."

"My Dad was like that, too," Shirley says. "Just didn't want to discuss it."

"Yup, Tommy's parents feel like the doctor's prying, asking them questions. That's the doctor's job, for God sake! I mean, the way his folks operate, they only give their doctor information on a need-to-know basis. Drives Tommy crazy."

"Still," Rita says, "we're lucky to still have them with us."

"That we are."

Celeste sighs, "I hate being an orphan," and Rita pats her hand.

Shirley adds, "As hard as it is with Mini sometimes, I'm glad to do it. We have some laughs, too, I gotta tell you."

"It's a gift, really. They were always there for us."

Shirley goes, "Certainly gives us something to yak about! Now top off my glass, will ya? And pass around those Marvelous whatevers."

"We may have to shut you off, Shirley," I says.

> *Yup, Tommy's parents feel like the doctor's prying, asking them questions. That's the doctor's job, for God sake!*

"Heck, I've only had a glass and a half of wine."

"No, I was talkin' about them Marcel Bars."

Recipes for Romance: Betty's Marvelous Marcel Bars

As I said, this is one of Betty's specialties, and is the next best thing to your Mom kissing your boo-boo. Don't know where exactly she got the recipe. I searched the internet, and come up with something called a Magic Cookie Bar which was close, but this is the way we make it up here in Mahoosuc Mills. I've included the recipe in this chapter because when the you-know-what hits the fan, you need at least one thing in your life that's marvelous! Plus, you only dirty one pan. How great is that?

Preheat the oven to 325 degrees. Get out your 13x9 glass pan. Melt one stick of butter in the pan by placing it in the oven. When it's melted, take out the pan and sprinkle 1½ cups graham cracker crumbs directly onto the butter. Kind of pat down a little. Pour on a can of Borden's Sweetened Condensed Milk. Next, sprinkle with an entire regular size bag of semi-sweet chocolate chips and, as if that wasn't enough, an entire regular size bag of peanut butter chips to finish. Bake for about 25 to 30 minutes. Cool, and enjoy!

What's Your Fallback Stress Position?

When stressed out, we all react in different ways: some folks run away, get overly busy, space out, or start cleaning the house, to name a few. I call this your fallback stress position. Knowing what you tend to do when stressed out will help you realize when it's happening, then you can act before things get outta hand.

When I hear myself say something like, "Look at all this junk mail!" Usually there's only a couple of pieces on the table, but to me it seems like a hundred, a sure sign I'm gettin' a little stressy. Or I start feeling overwhelmed by how messy the house is. I mean, it looks filthy and cluttered to me. Mind you, by most people's standards, it's pretty darn tidy. I'm Franco American after all, and keeping a clean house is in my blood. (My Mom had a special brush for combing the fringe of the area rugs so they lay just right.) But when I'm off my stride, all I can see are my shortcomings in the housekeeping department.

That's when I know I need to have a little conversation with myself. What's going on, Ida? What's bugging you? Can you do something about it? If so, do it. If it's outta your control, stop fretting and let it go.

Now, Charlie's fall back stress position is to zone out. He starts spending more time in his workshop or watching TV. He's not real chatty. When we first got married, I'd ask him what the matter was, which made matters worse. (He said that kinda made him feel smothered, so I learned to give the guy his space.) Nowadays, I let him be while he works things out in his own time. I trust that when he's ready to talk about it, he will.

The most important thing to remember when things go south is that everyone is doing their best. It might not look like it because it's not what you'd do in that situation, but give 'em the benefit of the doubt. Knowing what you and your spouses' fall-back stress positions are will help you be kinder to yourself and your loved one.

Straight Talk From the Barcalounger: When the Goin' Get's Tough, the Tough Hang Tight

In a marriage, you gotta have your eye on the long game, because not every season is a winning one. If you strike out in the third inning or she drops the ball at the top of the sixth, you may be tempted to quit playing altogether. But if you do, you're gonna miss that grand slam in the bottom of the ninth.

Ask yourself, am I in it to win it? If so, hang tight. Heck, I figure if I can stick with the Red Sox after all the grief they've given me over the years, I can certainly stand by my bride. Remember: this, too, shall pass, because it always does.

Love Mahoosuc Mills Style: The Little Things

This January was bitter cold in Mahoosuc Mills. It was sunny, but all that means is if you're inside, looking out, it's a beautiful day. When you're outside getting the mail or scraping the frost off your windshield, and you step back into your warm house, it makes you realize just how lucky you are.

In the dark and cold of January we have to look for the light where we can find it. For me, that means focusing on the little things I'm grateful for: that first sip of coffee in the morning, my electric blanket and flannel sheets, my healthy body as I hustle my butt from the car across the parking lot to the A&P in the freezing cold.

Looking for the little things gets me to slow down and really see what's around me, to appreciate instead of taking for granted. Sometimes I say "thank you" in my head (or out loud, if no one's around), or sometimes I just take a deep breath and smile. At things like Scamp, for instance.

Luckily, our little dog is like my gratitude savings account, he really is. If I'm having a bad day, just zoning in on him will make me feel better. God, he's some cute! Sometimes I'm talking to him, and he cocks his head and listens, you know, the way dogs do, and my heart just melts. Or maybe he's standing on his back legs, looking out the window, all wound up because the garbage truck is across the street like it is every Monday. It would be easy to get irritated at all the ruckus he's making, but if I stop and really look at him with his black button eyes open wide, his tail wagging, protecting our double wide, it's hard not to smile.

Or how about this: you use the last little bit on the roll of toilet paper, or your body wash gives a little squirt and then it's empty, or something like that, and you open the cabinet and get out another one because you planned ahead. How great is that? Or the smell of something cooking in the crockpot when I walk in the door. Reminds me of coming home as a kid to dinner cooking, my mother standing in the kitchen. Or biting into an exceptionally good Pink Lady apple, tart, sweet, and juicy. Wow! How about a hot shower? I mean, really taking the time to feel that hot water magically pouring down on you. Not everyone in the world gets to experience that. Or laughing so hard with my sister, I can't finish telling her what's so funny. Or, for me, every time someone comes up to me and says they like the stories I tell or advice I gave has made a difference in their lives.

Then there's Charlie, of course: taking out the trash without me having to ask. The way he smiles when Scamp jumps onto his lap and how patiently he sits there, petting him. How, when one of our electric Christmas candles for the window broke, and I sent him to get a new one and they were all out, he went to Smitty's Hardware and got what he needed to fix the one we had. For the rest of the season, every time I turned on that light, I said a little thank you. Charlie tuckin' into a dinner I made, knowing that even though he might not say so, he really loves it. In fact, sometimes, I look at Charlie while he's doing something, or even just watching TV, and I'm filled with gratitude because he's still my high school sweetheart!

Getting Goin'

- Ask yourself how you can be a better team player. It's about working with your (and your mate's) strengths, not against them.
- Is it time for the talk with your folks? Check out *The Conversation Project*.
- If you haven't already, work with your parents to get their paperwork in order and make a Go Kit with everything you'll need if something happens. While you're at it, put that medication list, doctors, and your contact numbers in an envelope and stick it on their fridge, clearly marked for the EMTs, just in case.
- When's the last time you talked to your folks? Or any of your older relatives. Call 'em up, take them out to lunch. Ask them about their life. You're lucky to have them.
- What's your fallback stress position? What's your husbands? Don't know? Make an effort to find out. Ask your spouse what they consider yours.
- If life's feeling a outta control or you're down in the dumps, look for the little things. Focusing on small things that are good will help you deal with the big things that aren't.

Nine

You Want Me to do What With Your Ashes?

L et your experience with your aging parents be motivation for you to take care of what you need to take care of. It's an act of love to plan for your happy old age.

Besides, if you take care of the big stuff, it'll free up time later. You know, so you can sit around with your friends and talk about how your kids are hinting that you should sign up for a Lifeline. And if God wanted you to get hearing aids, then why'd he put the volume button on the remote? Or giggling about how when you're with your kids, you pretend that you never use your cane. And you love the looks on their faces as you totter across the parking lot to Applebee's.

You don't want to miss out on that laugh riot. So, find a good lawyer and get your paperwork in order. Review it every time things change. You know the drill: will, living will, power of attorney, medical proxy.

And I can't stress this enough: This is no time to be a skinflint. Investing some money up front, will save you money in the end. And that includes looking at your finances, too. Yeah, I know you do your own taxes, blah, blah. But if you screw up on your Easy Tax, all you get is a slap on the wrist. If you drop the financial ball at this stage of the game, you're gonna end up eating cat food. If you're gonna do it, do it right.

Find a good financial planner. Ask your friends, your accountant, your doctor, anyone who seems good with money who they would recommend. Interview a minimum of three people. Your financial planner needs to be someone you're comfortable with, listens to you and your needs, and explains things in a way that doesn't bore you into a coma.

> *Your financial planner needs to be someone you're comfortable with, listens to you and your needs, and explains things in a way that doesn't bore you into a coma.*

Attend the planning session with your mate so you're both on the same page. Some possible questions that you might discuss are: Ideally, when would you like to retire? When you think about retirement, what kind of things do you picture yourself doing? Will we stay in our house, or move to Florida, or buy a camp? Do you picture us traveling or taking up a hobby? How important is it to leave something to our children?

Once you get the legal and financial stuff all taken care of, let your family members know your wishes, then you can get back to your bucket list. They may find it a little morbid, might not want to talk about it, but in the end, they will be thankful for your forethought. It's never to early to do this, because you never know.

Funeral Pictures and the Death Trunk

My parents put their stuff in order in their late fifties. My Aunt Alma had come for a visit and just dropped dead of a heart attack. Alma, my Mom's sister, was sixty-two years old, and just seven months from retirement. Mom and Aunt Alma planned to spend the day shopping, and Alma was getting ready downstairs. My parents' house had a finished basement with a bedroom and full bath. Well, Alma was taking her sweet time getting ready, so Mom hollered down: "What's takin' you so long, Alma? Are you dead or something?"

And I'll be darned. She was.

Alma never married and my mother was her only sibling. Mom, Dad, Irene, and me went down to Portland, where Alma worked as an office manager for an electrical contractor. We found her papers, planned a memorial service, cleaned out her apartment, and decided what the heck to do with all her stuff. Man, she had a lot of stuff!

> *Well, Alma was taking her sweet time getting ready, so Mom hollered down: "What's takin' you so long, Alma? Are you dead or something?" And I'll be darned. She was.*

That kind of shock sticks with you. So, once the dust settled, Mom and Dad did what they needed to do to spare Irene and me that kind of trumatic situation. They cleaned out their attic and garage. Got their paperwork in order and even planned their own funerals—chose the readings, songs, and the like.

Once all those necessary items were finished, Mom said to my Dad, "Let's go to the mall and have our funeral pictures taken while we still look good."

And they did.

Less than ten years later, my Mom was diagnosed with head and neck cancer. Over the next four and a half years, the doctors kept slicing away at her, but damn, when the time came, didn't she look good in that picture!

Now, back when Mom and Dad were getting their stuff in order (decluttering, we'd call it nowadays), they put together a special gift for Irene and me. I encourage you to do the same for your kids. We call it the Death Trunk, though you can probably come up with a better name. It was a trunk filled with momentos that meant something to Irene and me, special things to make us laugh and cry. We were supposed to look through it together after our parents were both gone.

So much for those plans. We opened the Death Trunk a little earlier than planned. When Dad was preparing to sell the house and move to Mahoosuc Green, we realized that there'd been water damage in the attic near the Death Trunk. He wasn't going to take the trunk (no room), so Irene and me decided to open it. We picked a Saturday morning to sort through it.

That trunk was plumb chucka full of memories. There were Irene's old marbles and a beat up, wooden Pinocchio marionette I used to play with. Our comic books and some elementary school report cards. Drawings of bumble bees and one of a tiger. A plastic change purse I loved and a scarf my sister had knit for her favorite doll. A photo of Irene and me having a Toni home perm. A needlepoint of some pansies with a little note pinned to it, "Can you believe your mother made this?"

That one did us in, and we had to take a chocolate break.

There were more rosary beads than you could shake a stick at, of course. But these ones were made special by the little notes (on yellow-lined paper and in Mom's handwriting) tucked inside the pouches. "Sterling silver beads we gave Aunt Alma for being in our wedding," one note read. There were a pair of well worn, dark wooden beads interlaced with a light pink crystal rosary and a slip of paper that read: "Grammy and Grampy's."

It was two years after she left this world, but it felt like we were talking with our Mom again. Irene and me divided up the treasure and brought it all downstairs. Dad had gotten some Italian sandwiches, BBQ chips, and soda for lunch. And there in the kitchen, we showed him our haul. That reminded Dad of some great stories, some of which I'd never heard. When I think back to that day with Death Trunk, sharing stories, laughing and crying with Irene, it always makes my heart sing.

Having the Talk

Of course, before you can discuss such things with your family, you must have the talk with your spouse. You're the one reading this book, so chances are you're the one who's gonna have to make it happen. Not everyone can play quarterback, remember? And apparently not everyone can be coach, secretary, and running back all in one. Suck it up. Waiting for him to bring it up is gonna make you crazy, so just muster your energy and drive it home.

I remember when I broached the subject with Charlie. Boy, I hadn't seen such enthusiasm since I told him we were going on the Cabbage Soup Diet.

"Geez Louise, Ida. Tell me you're not serious."

"I am, Charlie, and I'm not taking no for an answer. We need to get our papers in order and discuss what we each want if something happens."

"Nothings gonna happen."

"Charlie, something happens every time you go out with the boys. Need I remind you of the time . . . "

"No, no, I don't need reminding!"

"Well, this is what I want for my birthday. Along with all the other stuff you were gonna get me!"

That got a little smile outta him. "Okay," he sighs, "when do you want to do it? And don't say tonight."

"No, we're both best in the morning." (I'd thought this out.) "How about this Sunday I cook us up a nice breakfast, bacon, eggs, and homemade biscuits, and then we sit down and make a start. Sound good?"

"Well, actually, I was planning to clean out my workshop Sunday."

"Yeah, right. Pull the other one, will ya? The last time you cleaned out that workshop, Jimmy Carter was President."

"Ouch!"

"Charlie, there's never going to be the perfect time to talk about this stuff. But it has to be done. It's your choice: home-made biscuits with molasses or high fiber cereal and skim milk? For a week."

"Uh, how about door number three?"

"There is no door number three."

"Alright, alright. Homemade biscuits."

"Good. I'll pull together the stuff we're gonna need. In the meantime, start thinking about what you want."

"Won't matter to me, Ida. I'll be dead."

"Very funny!"

So, we had the talk. It went better than expected. I downloaded the starter kit for The Conversation Project. Charlie and me didn't exactly work through all the questions in the kit, though. I thought that might put Charlie off. I read it and sort of boiled it down for him. You know, the Cliff's Notes version.

Actually, there were a few surprises. Turns out, if it comes down to pulling the plug, Charlie doesn't care who does it. I mean, a complete stranger walking down the hall of the hospital, is fine with him, so long as it gets done.

Me, I want Charlie and Irene to make the decision together. That way Charlie will have someone to talk it over with. He won't feel so alone.

We both want to be cremated, but I don't really care what happens to my ashes. I figure they should be scattered someplace where folks who knew me can go and think of me every now and then.

But Charlie had other ideas.

"I want 'em scattered up on Ragged Mountain, overlooking Mount Katahdin," he said. "Great snowmobiling up there. Beautiful part of Maine. Nothing but wilderness as far as the eye can see. The boys'll know where."

"Yeah, but what if they're all gone, too?"

"I'll mark it on a map."

"Okay, let me get this straight. If you go before me, I gotta wait until winter, then suit up, and snowmobile into the wilds of Maine to scatter your ashes?"

"Yup, you'll have a great time."

"But hopefully, I'll be an old woman by then."

"Heck, if you're too old, you can just ride on a sled with one of the boys or get a guide. Ida, the view up there is . . . well, to die for."

149

Don't End Up in the Boonies, Unless You Want To

Is it time to downsize?

If you're "on the back nine" as Betty, who's a golfer, says (meaning you've lived more of your life than you have left), do you really want to spend your time and energy maintaining a house that no longer suits your lifestyle? Think about whether or not you really need all that room. I mean, how often do the kids really visit?

Before selling, you need to think it through and be absolutely clear about what you want and where you want to live. That way, you won't end up far from friends and family (unless, of course, that's what you want). Talk it out, write it down, and look at it often to remind yourself of what you're looking for. I don't know if you remember what it was like the last time you shopped for a house, but it's real easy to get caught up in the excitement. Before you know it, you've expanded your price range from what you want to pay to what you're "qualified" for. Or you're looking at places that are ten minutes or more outside where you wanted to be. The difference between being fifteen minutes outside of town and twenty-five minutes is huge!

Just last week, I saw Harriet Pierce down to the A&P. "Gee, Harriet," I say, "I haven't seen you down to the bean supper much lately. Are you going to the earlier seating?"

"Not going at all. You know we bought a condo up to Ellison Farm out on the Bennett Lot Road."

"I didn't. Congratulations! I heard those are beautiful. Got that little fish pond and everything."

"Oh, it's wonderful to have a smaller space, and brand new, too. Our old place was built in 1851, so it was always something."

"I hear you. Hard to keep up an old house. You must be loving it."

"That I am. Except it's just far enough out that once we're home, it's hard to psych ourselves up to head back into town in the evening."

"I'll bet you're so cozy there, you hardly miss it," I say. But what I'm thinking is: You couldn't pay me enough to live way out there. And what if something happens to her husband? She is stuck out in the boonies.

Not ready to downsize yet? Will you be in five years? Maybe ten? It's not too early to start decluttering and lightening your load. Do it now while you still have the energy. You're going to have to sort through things eventually, so why wait?

It's kind of liberating, really. And, as my niece Caitlin, who is a Feng Shui consultant, says, "You have to let go of the things you no longer want, in order to make room for new things you do."

Can't declutter because you're keeping a bunch of things for your kids after you're gone? It may be time to put together a Death Trunk (don't forget the little notes). If you are saving things for your kids that you're no longer using—give it to them now! That way you get the bonus of watching them enjoy it. And if you're storing stuff for your kids, honey, you're old enough to think about downsizing, so your kids are old enough to haul their own stuff around. Once it's their responsibility, it might become less precious to them (surprise, surprise), and they'll be ready to let some of it go.

The Mystery of the Pudgy Husband

Charlie went in for a physical a while back, and I guess he got a smack down by his doctor. Apparently, his weight was up and so was his blood pressure. His cholesterol's okay, but I'm thinking that's due more to heredity than clean living. And to be honest, Charlie was looking a little more portly than usual.

He doesn't eat that bad at home. Sure, we have our share of treats, especially when the Dairy Queen's open, but we were eating no worse than usual. So I gotta admit, I was a little perplexed.

"Charlie, what's going on?" I ask.

"Beats me, Ida. I think I'm just too short for my weight."

"You and me both, sweetheart. You haven't been eating anything different?"

"Nope!"

I wasn't buying it. Clearly, some detective work was in order. I'm no Sherlock Holmes, but common sense told me to start down to the Busy Bee. It's famous for Bud's Baked Bean Breakfast Buffet, served Thanksgiving through Christmas, as well as his wife Babe's homemade cinnamon rolls with maple icing. Oh, and I can't forget her bacon biscuits with the cream cheese filling.

Off I went to the Busy Bee, ordered up a bacon and cream cheese biscuit and a cup of coffee—just to be polite. Besides, detective work is tiring, and I needed to keep up my strength.

Small talk outta the way, I got down to business. "Babe, has Charlie been in here more than usual, lately?"

"Oh, Ida," Babe says, smiling, "you know I can't tell you that. What happens down to the Busy Bee, stays down to the Busy Bee."

"I know, Babe, and I wouldn't ask you to break your code unless it was a matter of life and death."

Sure I was laying it on thick, but I needed an answer.

"Goodness, Ida, what is it?"

"Well," I explained, "Charlie's weight and his blood pressure are up, and I'm getting a little concerned about it."

"Gee, I'm sorry to hear that, Ida. But Charlie hasn't been in much lately. Just every now and then for a cup of coffee. I think the last time he had a Big Boy was on his birthday, with you."

"Weird. Well, thanks anyway, Babe!"

I had to get to work, but frankly, if I couldn't get any answers at the Busy Bee, the trail was already cold. Babe knows about everything going on in Mahoosuc Mills and then some.

Next time I saw them, I brought it up to the Women Who Run With the Moose, and Celeste said that, come to think of it, Bud was also looking a little bigger around the middle.

"Junior's been pudging out, big time," Shirley chimed in.

"Hmm, the plot thickens!"

So, a week later, I'm opening up my register down to the A&P when Babe comes in, a huffin' and puffin'.

"Ida!" she gasps, "I think I know what's causing Charlie to pork out."

I flicked off my register light. "Do tell!"

"Pumpkin's been into the Busy Bee," (Pumpkin is our fire chief), "and he told me I can't bring any more donuts over to the fire house."

"Why?"

"Because he says his volunteer firemen are getting too fat to fit through windows."

Light dawns on Marble Head.

"I wondered why Charlie was spending so much time down to the engine house. Figured they were just spiffing up the fire truck for the Fourth of July parade."

"Oh, it's all my fault. I've been working on this new recipe for maple-glazed bacon donuts."

"Hold on a minute, here. Did you say maple-glazed bacon donuts?"

I put my hand over my fluttering heart, and I do believe I heard angels sing.

"Yup, and I needed some taste testers. Charlie and all them guys down to the fire department volunteered. It's taken awhile to perfect the recipe, so for weeks now I've been bringing a couple dozen donuts down to the fire station on weekends. I guess the guys have been scarffing them down."

"Well, who wouldn't, Babe?"

"Anyways, thought I'd better fess up. You can stop worrying about Charlie. Pumpkin's banned the donuts from the engine house, and says he's gonna make the guys do a little work out boot camp in the fall. When the weather cools down."

"Thanks, Babe, mystery solved."

"Oh, here," she says, handing me a little bakery bag. "I brought you one, to say I'm sorry. This version's going on the menu."

Let me just say, that maple-glazed bacon donut was so sinfully good, I practically needed a cigarette after, and I don't even smoke!

 ## Recipe For Romance: Be Sneaky

Fried bologna, anyone? Maybe a Vienna Sausage sandwich made with yellow mustard on Wonder Bread? How about some baked Spam? All used to be favorites early in our relationship, but things change. Though I gotta admit, every once in a while I do throw together some crushed pineapple, brown sugar, a little mustard, and a small onion, and pour it on top of some Spam, bake until it's golden brown and bubbly. But that's a special treat, and the next morning I have to take an extra water pill.

Despite an occasional flirtation with maple-glazed bacon donuts, Charlie and me are really trying to eat healthier. If you want a happy old age together, it's part of the deal. Charlie's not too fussy when it comes to food and he doesn't mind leftovers. Thank God! Don't get me wrong, we're not going to start Vegan Tuesdays anytime soon. If it doesn't have meat, Charlie doesn't considered it a meal. Period.

Charlie's not fussy, but I still need to sneak in some healthy stuff where

> *Don't get me wrong, we're not going to start Vegan Tuesdays anytime soon. If it doesn't have meat, Charlie doesn't considered it a meal. Period.*

I can. I cook with olive oil instead of butter, put veggies into the spaghetti and meat sauce (though whole wheat noodles are a no-go). I use leaner beef and pork, fix a salad at dinner with a lowfat dressing. Leave the skins on the new potatoes and switched to whole wheat bread instead of the white stuff. I try to make a fruit salad every couple of weeks, and sweeten it with a little maple syrup. Charlie won't eat fruit in its natural state, but somehow, if I cut it up and add syrup, it's more appealing (go figure!).

I haven't had much success getting him to drink more water (but I'm drinking enough for the two of us) or banning junk food from the house. What fun would that be? But I have started putting the Doritos, nuts, and ice cream in a small bowl and leaving the bag, jar, or container in the kitchen. If he wants more, he can get it himself, which he doesn't seem all the motivated to do, so he's eating less of it. Same with our meals. I plate 'em up and leave the extras on the counter and stove. Laziness is a weight loss tool!

When we go to the mall or a restaurant or something, I always have him park far from the entrance. We started that when he got his new truck (you know, so it wouldn't get dinged up), and it's kind of stuck. On the weekend, if the weather's good, I walk with Charlie and Scamp first thing. That way, we go a little further than if he was by himself.

These don't seem like big changes, but they add up. Taking care of yourself heath-wise is another way of showing up in your marriage.

Straight Talk From the Barcalounger: We've Had a Good Run

I have been plowing snow and mowing lawns long as I can remember. Used to do it as a kid to make money. When we first got the double-wide, I took pride in keeping the yard up and making sure the driveway was clear of the white stuff. I've graduated from shoveling to snowblower to plow, from push mower to rider to zero turn. Every time I get a new toy, it perks up my interest.

But frankly, I'm looking forward to hanging up my jersey. Especially after the winters we've had lately. Even with a plow, you gotta snowblow the paths to the door and for the oil guy, shovel out the mailbox, clear off the deck, and rake the roof. The zero turn makes short work of the yard, but to be honest, me and my weed wacker don't always get along. It's what you might call "temperamental."

I don't want to give up the double-wide or nothing. Not ready for Mahoosuc Green just yet. But I sure am ready to get rid of the gottas—gotta do this, gotta do that. I'm looking forward the wannas. I wanna kick back with a Bud on the deck; I wanna putter in my workshop; I wanna watch a game on the weekend without feeling guilty because I should be outside doing chores. Me and my toys have had a good run, but the thrill is gone!

Love Mahoosuc Mills Style: Let Him Retire First

Bud was the first of our little group to retire. He worked for Gagne's & Sons Heating and Cooling for thirty-plus years. That's dirty work, repairing furnaces and the like. Plus, you get called out at all hours, day and night. Weekends, too, don't matter the weather. And unless you're doing an annual cleaning, the people you're dealing with are usually upset. I mean, it's ten degrees out, and no heat. They're all bundled up, seeing their breath inside the house, and Bud's gotta be the one who tells them their furnance is shot. No fun. Once he hit sixty-five, Bud was outta there.

When he started talking about retiring, I says to Celeste, "Are you turning in your papers, too?" She's a school secretary. Worked her way up from elementary school to the superintendent's office.

"Nope."

"Geez, Celeste, you must have enough time in."

"I do. Twenty-seven years, now."

"Do you love it that much?"

"Well, it's a decent job. Benefits and hours are great. Makes me feel useful. But that's not the reason I'm staying."

"What, then?"

"Well, if I retire the same time as Bud, he'll be underfoot all the time. You know, always on me: 'What are we doing today? What are we having for lunch?' Don't get me wrong,

I love him to death. But I just couldn't take twenty-five or so years of that."

"I hear you."

"This way, he'll get into his own routine. It'll be up to him to figure out how to plan his day. I figure he'll sit around doing nothing for a few weeks, then he'll get bored. Maybe start volunteering down to the Senior Center, taking folks to the doctor, picking up prescriptions. Or, do a little snow plowing on the side, get a hobby. You know, start playing golf or something. He's gonna be more motivated if I'm not around."

Far as the old gals down to the Senior Center are concerned (and I know this almost first hand because Irene told me), the sun rises and sets on Bud.

"You're wicked smart, Celeste."

"I try. But to be honest, I'm pretty motivated, myself. Listen, when I retire, I wanna do what I wanna do, okay? Sure, we'll travel and spend time together. But you and me know that being with your husband 24/7 is just too much of a good thing."

"Ain't that the truth!"

And you know what? Her strategy worked like a charm. Far as the old gals down to the Senior Center are concerned (and I know this almost first hand because Irene told me), the sun rises and sets on Bud. Well, he's so good with 'em, and you can tell he really likes helping them out. No more, "Mr. Bad News Bud." Plus, he's not coming home filthy every day. Can't beat that!

Senior Tattoos and Ensure Tastings

There are many ways you can plan for a happy old age, and keeping your friendships strong is one of them. I'm reminded of that every time I spend time with the Women Who Run With the Moose.

Us girls get together once a week for a little girl time, but when it's one of our birthdays, we do something special. The birthday gal gets to choose what. Lots of times it involves a field trip. My last birthday was a big one, so I decided that what I really wanted was a good ol' fashioned birthday party, just us gals.

"I'll host," Rita says, "but it'll be more fun if we have a theme."

"How about an Ensure tasting?" Shirley quips.

"What's that?" Rita asks.

"Kind of like a wine tasting, for the elderly!"

"You oughta know, Shirley," I say. "Seeing you're three months older than me!"

"How about a Botox party?"

"Walker and cane demonstration?"

"We could chip in and buy Ida one of them walkers with the seat for when she gets tired," Betty says, cracking herself up. "Decorate it for her."

"I'll crochet a little bag to put on the front, for her to put stuff in."

"Streamers for the handlebars."

"Very funny," I manage to squeeze in, because those gals were on a roll. "Here's what I'm thinking: a 'Pamper Yourself Party.'"

Betty jumps in, "Oh, I like that! We could do mud masks, hand scrubs."

"Foot soaks with scented bath salts!" Rita adds.

"Okay, okay," goes Shirley. "But let's talk about the important stuff—food! What do you want to eat, Ida? And what kind of cake?"

"No cake, no entrees. I just want appetizers and desserts. And ice cream—gobs and gobs of ice cream."

"And drinks," Dottie says. "We're gonna need libations, you know, to help us relax."

"We're on it, Ida. When?" Betty asks.

"Well," I says, "it'll have to be a Friday night, because all that pampering is bound to reek havoc with my hair. Patsy down to Hair Affair will put it to rights on Saturday morning."

"It's a plan!"

Once that was settled, we moved on to the next topic, and the next, like you do with good friends. Dot had been in for a physical. The whole "lube, oil, and filter" as Shirley calls it.

"God, don't they ask you a lot of questions," she says. "Took me forever to fill out the form. How much caffeine am I drinking? What am I doing to de-stress. How am I sleeping? How much do I poop and when?"

> *Took me forever to fill out the form. How much caffeine am I drinking? What am I doing to de-stress. How am I sleeping? How much do I poop and when?*

"Did they ask you how often you and Tommy do the deed?" Celeste asks.

"Of course."

"Who does the doctor think she is, anyways? Masters and Johnson?" Shirley chimes in.

"What'd you tell her, Dottie?" I tease.

"I said, 'About average for a couple that's been together for over forty years: New Years Eve, Tommy's birthday, Fourth of July and Veteran's Day.'"

"Not Arbor Day?"

"Nope, easier to just plant a tree."

Well, that got us going.

Rita says, "Know what question I hate? Date of your last period."

"Really!" Dot agrees. "How am I supposed to remember that? It's gotta be over ten years."

"Yeah, don't they have it in their files some place?"

"After a certain age, they should just stop asking you that."

"Should," I says, "but they won't. We'll be checking into the Alzheimer's wing at Mahoosuc Green, and someone'll still want to know the date of our last period."

"Right! And at that point, we'll be lucky if we remember our own names."

Betty goes, "I know! Maybe we should just get the date of our last period tattooed on our arm. 'Let me check,' you say. Then you roll up the sleeve of your cardigan and voila, there it is."

"Why stop there?" says Celeste, rolling up the sleeve of her other arm. "Father's middle name."

Shirley lifts her pant leg, "Mother's maiden name? Right here!"

"Last four digits of my social?"

"Oh, gotta protect that."

"How about on my stomach, upside down so only I can read it?"

"Pin number?"

"I'm gonna need a mirror for that one because it's written backwards on my butt!"

By now we're almost peeing our pants, we're laughing so hard. Tears streaming down our faces.

"Shirley!" I says, "Speaking of doctors, have you scheduled your colonoscopy yet?"

"Yeah, it's only ten years overdue!"

"Nope, like I've said many times before, it's nobody's business what's up there but my own!"

And with that, I think at least one of us did pee our pants!

Getting Goin'

- Have the talk with your mate, and let your family know your wishes.
- Write your obituary and pick out your funeral photo.
- Get your finances in order.
- Start working on a Death Trunk for your loved ones.
- What house chores are you ready to get rid of? Make a list, and try to let go of at least one thing.
- If you're ready to downsize, write down exactly what you're looking for and where you want to be.
- Plan a yard sale and start the decluttering process. Use the money you make to pay for some of the expert advice you might need in the future.
- Is it time to schedule a colonoscopy and/or a mammogram? Have you gotten your shingles vaccine? Make the call and get it on the calendar. Do what you need to do to be healthy for yourself and your spouse.
- Make a standing date with a friend or two. When you get together, bring your calendar and ink in your next date before you part ways.

Ten

The Last One Standing

You can't help but think about it. Unless the two of you are in a plane crash or something, chances are, one of you is gonna be the last one standing. And, if you're like me, you don't know which is worse: dying first, and making your husband go through that trauma, or him going first and being left all by your lonesome to pick up the pieces. Good thing it's outta our hands, right?

There's other kinds of leaving, too. I know from watching my mother go through her cancer journey, your loved one can still be here sitting with you, but you're actively missing the healthy person they once were. Same with dementia (or "old timers" as my cousin Mikey calls it). The person you love is with you, but not *with* you. Hard, either way.

Then there's divorce. Lately, I've been hearing more about this: people divorcing in their fifties and sixties. I guess once the kids have flown the coop, you wake up one day and realize, Whoa! Who is this stranger I'm married to? This is not quite the future you planned when you walked down the aisle.

163

Whether your mate dies, gets sick, drifts away or leaves, you've suffered a loss—and losses have to be grieved. If you don't take time to mourn, believe me, it'll come back and bite you in the bum. There are no short cuts. The only way of getting through grief is to grieve.

Why Get Outta Bed in the Morning?

After you lose someone, there's still this blissful feeling when you first wake up—for just a minute—you're hopeful about the new day, you feel rested and energized. It doesn't last. It's a mirage. A dark cloud quickly rolls in from outta nowhere. Your heart hurts and your stomach churns. You have this woozy kind of elevator dropping sensation, and, just like that, you remember that your life has changed—forever. In the snap of a finger, just getting outta bed, which had seemed so easy, is now nearly impossible.

> *Your heart hurts and your stomach churns. You have this woozy kind of elevator dropping sensation, and, just like that, you remember that your life has changed—forever.*

But you do get outta bed. And you do it the way you do everything now—one little step at a time. You roll over on your side. You fold back the covers. You take a deep breath. You take another deep breath. Maybe you sit there for a bit, just staring blankly into space. You finally let out a deep sigh and stand up. You repeat this day after day, and slowly, it gets a little easier. It doesn't go away, but it gets easier.

It helps if you have a reason to get up and dressed. After my mother died, my father started buying groceries one day at a time. It got him out of the house and out among people.

Sometimes, he'd go to the mall and walk or drink a coffee sitting in the food court.

"The hardest time is in the evening," he told me. "I'm pretty good all day, but after supper is hard."

Dad has always read the newspaper first thing in the morning as long as I can remember, but he started saving it until after dinner. "Gives me something to look forward to," he said.

My advice is to talk to someone. Your best bet is folks who've gone through the same thing. Could be a friend who's lost a spouse or a support group of some sort. This is especially helpful if your spouse is suffering from dementia or another chronic illness. Grieving groups are really wonderful, too, because after awhile, you just don't want to burden your family, but you still need to talk. The people in these groups understand because they're going through the same thing. A grieving group is a safe place where you can get it all out, and that includes talking about how mad you are at your spouse for deserting you, damn it!

A Beautiful Day

It's a beautiful day here in Mahoosuc Mills: high seventies, no humidity, sun shining, birds singing. I'm sitting at my computer thinking about what to write, when across the street, I see two men wheeling a stretcher to the Phinney's front door. Weird! Never heard an ambulance. But as I look more closely, I see there's a body bag on the stretcher. My heart sinks as I realize—Lois has finally died, poor dear.

> *Weird! Never heard an ambulance. But as I look more closely, I see there's a body bag on the stretcher. My heart sinks as I realize— Lois has finally died, poor dear.*

She's been in the process of dying for weeks now from lung cancer. Lois smoked her whole life. Her husband, Roger, didn't though, and he did his darndest to get her to stop. She tried, but it never took. Cars have been coming and going all week as folks checked in, family visited, and hospice workers went about their business.

The door opens and they're wheeling out the stretcher. For a minute I think maybe they're just taking Lois back to the hospital to drain the fluid from her lungs. Maybe an ambulance has been hiding behind that big maple tree all this time. But then I see the way her son Bob is standing there, back stiff, hands crossed in front, and I know there's no ambulance.

Just then it pops into my head how September 11, 2001 was a beautiful day, too, just like this one. When I finally had the strength of will to shut off the TV that day, I went outside and threw the ball for our dog at the time, Belle. Over and over, I'd toss it, and she'd bring it back, tail wagging, no idea what had just happened. Sun shining, birds singing . . .

Becky, Lois and Roger's oldest child, wanders out, looking lost. She has Down syndrome. She's in her forties and lives with her parents. "She's my gift," Lois used to say. "I don't know what I'd do without her." Becky stands there for a bit, weight shifting from foot to foot, then turns and goes back inside, screen door slamming.

Scamp hears the slam, runs to our screen door, standing on his back legs. I snap, "Scamp, don't you dare bark!"

As I watch them put Lois into the back of a black SUV, I flashback to another beautiful, unseasonably warm October day—the day my own mother passed away. The stretcher, the body bag, discussing which door would be best for going in and out. My sister Irene and our Dad couldn't do it, so I ended up opening and closing the door. I opened and closed the back gate as Mom left our house one final time.

Across the street, the SUV slowly drives away. Bob starts to wave good-bye, thinks better of it, and lets his arm drop to his side. He stands there a minute, his body sagging. Then Bob straightens, turns, walks back up the path and disappears inside.

Next door to the Phinney's someone is using a weed wacker. The droning of it won't let up, and I'm thinking, Lois has just died. Have some respect!

But that's the thing: life goes on, right? This fella's still wacking weeds as Jim Blais, owner of Blais's Funeral Home, returns with a portfolio under his arm. So many decisions to make, things to organize, details to take care of. If you've never been through it, it can seem overwhelming. But believe me, it can also be nice to have something to do, something else to think about. Any kind of a diversion is welcome, really.

I start thinking about what I'll make to bring over to the Phinney's for Roger, Bob, and Becky. The weed wacker drones, and cars keep passing by. The hanging pink petunia plant by the Phinney's front door is still gorgeous. It's a beautiful day here in Mahoosuc Mills.

No Regrets

It's been twelve and a half years since my mother passed away, the conclusion of a four-year cancer journey, as the folks at hospice call it. What a roller coaster ride. Just thinking about it still makes me dizzy.

When Mom was sick, Dad, Irene and me had a little thing we kept saying to each other: No regrets. Our feeling was that grieving was going to be hard enough. Why muddy it up with regrets?

> *No regrets. Our feeling was that grieving was going to be hard enough. Why muddy it up with regrets?*

If a little voice in my head said, "Call the doctor and ask him if there's anything more we can do about the pain," I called. If Mom mentioned how she might like to go strawberry picking, off we went. A lobster dinner? Sure! We talked to her about her life, told her what a great mother she was. We asked her if she was scared. Tough conversations, but in the long run it was a lot better than carrying around a truck load of regrets.

One thing I don't regret is signing Mom up for hospice. I can't say enough about the wonderful folks there: Maureen, our visiting nurse; Carol, our social worker; and Maya, the hospice chaplain. What a team!

People think hospice is just for people on death's door, but that's not true. And hospice is not just for cancer, either. Could be your loved one has ALS or dementia or something like that. Basically, if there's nothing more the medical folks can do for you or you've decided you're done with treatment, hospice comes to your rescue. You're not giving up. You'd just rather enjoy what time you have left instead of having chemo again and being sick as a dog to get maybe an extra couple of months. As they say, "Hospice is about caring, not curing." They help manage the pain, arrange for things like hospital beds, and have someone bathe the sick person a couple times a week. They coach your family on how to care for your loved one. Your social worker or chaplain is there to talk to everyone involved, not just with the person who's sick. They educate the family about what to expect and how best to help.

And that's the thing about hospice, it's about providing support for the whole family. It doesn't end after your loved one is gone, either. You can call hospice and they'll come help you do what you need to do. They'll dispose of medications and help you get rid of medical equipment. And they lead grieving groups.

I know this from being with my Mom: helping your loved one die with dignity is a privilege. It's a starkly beautiful event. Being with her when she passed, it was like my Mom gave birth to me again. I know Dad and Irene felt it, too. It changes you, in a good way.

Life After the Titanic

Dottie is a big fan of anything to do with the Titanic. Not just the movies, but books, too. Especially books that deal with what happened to the survivors.

"What do you like about these books, Dottie?" I asked. "Isn't it kind of depressing?"

"Just the opposite. It's fascinating to see how people deal with a tragedy like that."

"How so?"

"Well, they fall into two categories, Ida," she says. "The people who feel so guilty about surviving that they can't keep it together. They just fall apart, some slow and some fast. Basically their spirit died on that ship, even though their body was rescued. Then there's the folks who believe they were spared for a reason. They go on to accomplish big things in the world, to touch people and make a difference. I'm not saying it was easy for them, but somehow they move forward. It's inspiring!"

> *Then there's the folks who believe they were spared for a reason. They go on to accomplish big things in the world, to touch people and make a difference.*

You hear about survivor guilt when it comes to war and major catastrophes, but not so much when it comes to losing your mate. But it's real, and knowing that can help you deal with it. Grieving is an ongoing process and it's different for everyone. You never really stop missing your mate, but take your time, feel the feelings, be kind to yourself and eventually, you'll realize that you're starting to move forward. It's not like nothing happened, but you're starting to discover your new normal.

This is where the "There Is No I in Team, but Maybe There Should Be" chapter pays off. You have a circle of friends in place, which is helpful. Maybe you start reading books again. You couldn't read while your mate was sick, you just couldn't concentrate. Start out with something light, no big complicated plot. Is there a hobby you've lost track of or want to try for the first time, like knitting or genealogy? Give it a go. Maybe there's an adult ed class you wanna take. It'll get you out with other people without having to interact in the same way you do at a party. Plus, hanging out with strangers may be easier right now because they don't look at you with pity.

Once you're able to be more social, try doing things with a group. My Dad started going to the dances down to the Elks. He sits with a table of friends, some couples and some singles. He also took up bowling. He goes twice a week. "I'm not much of a bowler, but it's a nice group of folks, and we have lunch after," he says.

I remember about six weeks after my mother died, there was a ham supper down to the church. Dad, Irene, and me decided to sign up as volunteers in honor of Mom. Folks at the church had been so wonderful, bringing over casseroles, checking in on Dad. Pitching in and helping others made the three of us feel better. It was amazing, really, how good it felt. That day was the first time since she passed that I saw a little bitty spark inside my Dad start to rekindle.

Recipe For Lack of Romance: The Healing Touch

It's curious, and not something you really think about in advance, but one of the hardest things about losing your mate is not being touched. All of a sudden, there may be these long stretches of time when no one touches you.

The good news is, there's an easy fix. Remember—look good, smell good, feel good. Ladies, make an appointment for a massage. Or have a manicure or pedicure or both. With a mani-pedi, you get the benefit of adding some color to your life. Freshly painted fingers and toes can really perk you up. Or, get your hair done. Maybe it's even time for a new do.

Guys, you can splurge and go to a barber who'll wash your hair and maybe give you a shave. You know, with that hot towel on your face and everything? Heck, go the whole nine yards. It will feel relaxing and after you'll feel better about yourself. Get your eyebrows trimmed (nose and ears, too, if they'll do it). Getting spiffed up will raise your spirits.

Or, how about this: take dancing lessons! I don't care what kind of music. You'll meet new people, stumble around a bit together, touch and be touched, and have fun. What the heck!

Cuddle with your pet. Hug a family member. Every little bit helps. Being hugged isn't going to make life go back to how it used to be, but it'll certainly make you feel a little better. Promise!

Straight Talk From the Barcalounger: Help a Widow Out

Once you get to a certain age, you realize folks in your own generation are passing away. You start looking at that lone geezer ferrying around a car load of widows, and you think—that might be me.

Now's the time to pay it forward, guys. If you know someone who's lost their husband, volunteer to help her out. I'm hoping someone will do that for Ida if I go happy trails before her. This might mean stacking some wood or putting together a shelving unit, clearing brush, or fixing a leaky faucet. Just a couple hours every now and then can really make a difference.

But if you're still happily married, bring along a friend. Who knows, maybe they'll hit it off!

Love Mahoosuc Mills Style: Making Him Proud

I was down to the Wally Mart with my friend Celina a while back. Since her husband, Henry, died, we try to get together once a month. Celina was looking for a new lipstick, and I was acting as her beauty consultant, you know, providing moral support.

Charlie and me had a special bond with Celina and Henry, because like us, they never had children. We did a lot of things together, as couples, especially in our twenties and thirties when most folks our age were busy with their kids.

They were a little older than us, and when Henry took early retirement from Central Maine Power, they became snowbirds, spending half their time in Florida.

It broke my heart when Henry got sick. I can't stand to see people suffer. He was a fighter, though. When he became housebound, I'd go visit once a week, bring a little treat for him to eat, free Celina to go run an errand or two.

Forty-five years, that's how long they were married. And they still acted like newlyweds. Henry called her his "bride," and Celina referred him as "my Henry." "My Henry" did this, "my Henry" said that. It would have been obnoxious if they weren't so cute.

At the wake, Celina says to me, "Ida, I still have the dress I wore to our thirtieth anniversary party. My Henry loved me in that dress. That's what I want to be buried in, so I look pretty when he sees me in heaven. You have to promise me you'll make sure they bury me in that dress. I've gained a little weight since then, so just slice it up the back."

Spending time with Celina, seeing her without her Henry, always makes me hug Charlie a little tighter when I get home. Sure, he may get on my nerves from time to time, but truth is, I just can't picture life without him.

Four years on, Celina's bounced back better than I would have thought. We grow 'em tough up here in the North Country! I remember having coffee with her a few months after Henry passed, and Celina says to me, tears in her eyes, "I feel so lost, Ida. I don't even know who I am without my Henry."

"Your Henry was a hell of a guy. Never complained. Even that last time when I brought him my special vanilla pudding. Though he did take his oxygen mask off and ask me for a cigarette."

"He was a rascal!"

"That he was. Are you sleeping better?"

"You know, I think I am. Turns out, I like going to bed a little later than Henry did, and I let myself sleep in a bit in the morning, too."

> *"After they die, your world expands again, but all that new time and space can feel kind of intimidating. You have to kind of grow into it."*

"It must be strange, rediscovering what you like and what you don't like."

"It is. But I find it less lonesome than keeping everything the same. Like I've been eating lots of broccoli lately, if you can believe it. Henry didn't like it, and now I can't get enough."

That's when I knew Celina would be all right. As much as she missed him, she was starting to rebuild her routine and I didn't get the sense that it made her feel disloyal to him. Celina's still got a tinge of sadness around her eyes, but she laughs more now. And she's got a great way of looking at things.

"You know, Ida, as your husband gets sicker, their world gets smaller, and so does yours. After they die, your world expands again, but all that new time and space can feel kind of intimidating. You have to kind of grow into it. It took me awhile, but if I can do it, anyone can. Of course, I have Henry egging me on. Sitting around feeling sorry for myself would be a disservice to his memory, and not what he'd want me to do. I still love him, Ida, and I want to make my Henry proud."

Celina's joined a book group and is active at the Senior Center. She goes on field trips with 'em, down to the big flower show in Portland, to the art museum, and she has a season ticket to the theater.

So, after our successful outing at the Wally Mart (I found a nice pink nail polish, and Celina got a lipstick in the prettiest shade of coral), we went to the DQ to celebrate. Over Peanut Buster Parfaits, Celina confided, "Ida, last night, I had a revelation. Made me feel a little guilty."

"Really, Celina? Do tell!"

"Well, you know how much I miss my Henry, right?"

"Goes without saying."

"Okay. So last night I'm standing in the bathroom, checking my eyebrows for stray hairs, putting on my night cream, flossing my teeth, when I hear a strange noise. Turns out, it's me, humming. I look at myself in the mirror, and I'm smiling. And at that moment, I realize: I miss my Henry in every room of this house, except here."

"In the bathroom?"

"Yup! Ida, I confess. I just love having a sink to myself."

"The stuff of dreams, Celina. It's the stuff of dreams!"

Getting Goin'

- Have you lost your spouse through death or divorce? Or are they sick, physically or mentally, and seem far away? Take the time you need to grieve.

- If your spouse is ill, calling hospice sooner, rather than later, is not giving up. It's about getting the support you need when you need it most.

- Talking to someone helps. Call a friend who's lost their mate and commiserate. Join a support group if your mate is still around and failing, or a grieving group if they've passed on. If you think you're too private to talk about it, go to another town and join there. They'll be strangers, so what the heck. And you don't have to talk. Just go and listen.

- How can you rebuild your day to make it work for you now? Sometimes trying to keep everything the same will just make you miss your mate more. Find at least one

thing you can do every day that will make you get up, get
dressed, and get outta the house.

- Once you're up for it, look for ways to be more social.
  Take a class, have lunch down to the Senior Center or try
  a new hobby.
- Make an appointment for a massage, mani-pedi, or to get
  your hair done. Guys, go to the barber and have your hair
  washed, maybe get a shave.
- Your spouse wouldn't want you to stop living. Make 'em
  proud by living life to the fullest. It's what you would
  want for them, right?

Eleven

Jumping Into the Deep End

You lost your spouse. You're still grieving, but some time has passed, and you feel the need for a little companionship. Nothing wrong with that. In fact, it's a good thing. Let me assure you, you're not being disloyal to your mate. You're doing what they would want you to do—moving forward with your life.

But how, right? Because you haven't dated since the Paleozoic era, and things have changed. The world is not the same place, and your body, well, let's just say you'd only consider doing the dance of the seven veils with eight veils.

Dating in your fifties, sixties, and (God bless you) your seventies and eighties might not be so much like tackle football as touch football. Heck, maybe it isn't football at all, but croquet, which is a fun game and, under the right circumstances, you can still work up a sweat doing it.

And more good news: at this point in your life dating is easier in some ways. You don't have all those hormones getting in the way of good choices. You're more comfortable in yourself and your life, and hopefully, you care less what people think. You have friends and family, hobbies and groups you belong to.

(If your spouse is still alive and kicking, don't skip this chapter. Some of the things I talk about here will help you in the dating your mate department. Heck, a lot of the makeover advice will just plan make you feel good. Now, that's a win/win!)

Laying a Good Foundation

Whether you're ready to start dating or not, your world has probably been on hold since your spouse passed and maybe for years before that, if they suffered through a long illness. Now, it's time to release the hold button, freshen things up, and expand your horizons. Trust me, it'll change your outlook on things. Here's the deal: you're not spiffing yourself up to attract a mate (though it might happen). You're doing it for yourself. Look good, smell good, feel good, right?

> *There's nothing romantic about prehistoric briefs, full of holes, stained, so ratty that your wife wouldn't even have used 'em as dust rags!*

As I said in Chapter 2, laying a good foundation is key, and by that I mean lingerie, underwear, whatever you want to call it. First off, go through your stuff and throw out anything that you wouldn't want someone else to see. This includes you guys, too. There's nothing romantic about prehistoric briefs, full of holes, stained, so ratty that your wife wouldn't even have used 'em as dust rags! She probably took care of this kind of thing, but now you have to step up to the plate. This is not just for looks, but it's practical, too.

Last winter, after one of our many big snow storms, I noticed it took Charlie forever to snowblow the driveway. A couple of hours later, he clomps back into the house. I'm making him some hot cocoa, because that's what you do when your husband's been out snowblowing. I says to him, "Is something wrong with the blower?"

"No, why?"

"Well, you kept stopping and disappearing into the shed."

"Naw," he says. "It's my underwear."

"Your underwear?"

"Elastic's shot. Had to keep going in there to pull 'em up."

"Why didn't you just come inside and change them?"

"I was all dressed. Take too long."

"Well, you must have had an inkling when you put them on this morning."

"Ya, but I was in a hurry to get out there. Besides, they're all shot, so it's slim pickings."

"Why don't you just buy some new underwear? I can't believe you let yourself suffer like that."

"Haven't gotten around to it. But I got a birthday coming up. Maybe I'll get my wife on it."

Keepin' the Girls Where They Belong

Gals, they say that you should get measured for a new bra once a year, and the older I get, the more I know that this is true. Because that ol' plumpness that was keeping the girls from heading south has been jumping ship at an alarming rate, and taking my cleavage with it!

Now as a rule, I like to shop with my sister or girl friends, but finding a new bra, that's a solo thing. It's serious business and takes concentration and fortitude. It's not about browsing around, talking, laughing, having a good time. No, you've got to stay focused. In my opinion, shopping for a bra is right up there with shopping for a bathing suit. Both score very low on the fun-o-meter.

But awhile back, I had this coupon and it needed to be done. I says to myself, "Self, you gotta man up!" I popped a couple of Hershey's Kisses (purely for medicinal purposes), and off I go to Victoria's Secret.

I wanted someone to measure and wait on me, like how it was in the olden days. You know, grandmotherly old ladies wearing bifocals, with tape measures around their necks, who give you two bra styles to try on, wait until you're undressed, then whip back the curtain and say, "How you doing, dear?" But that, my friends, is in a galaxy far, far away. And Victoria's Secret is an alternate universe.

Did you see the movie *Invasion of the Body Snatchers*? Charlie and me caught that one at the drive-in. Well, that's what the sales girls look like at Victoria's Secret. That or like the *Stepford Wives*. They all look the same: tight, black clothes, long, straightened hair, a ton of make-up, and a little too much perfume, if you ask me. And they're wired up to the Mother Ship, talking into their lapels.

So I walk in, and a sales girl ("Brooke", it says on her name tag) asks, "Can I help you?"

"Yeah, I'd like to get measured for a new bra."

"Great!" she says, and Brooke instructs me to go out back, where Heather will fix me up.

Out back, I find a gal who is Heather, but who looks an awful lot like a Brooke. She asks me what size bra I'm wearing? I tell her, but she measures me anyway, and I wonder if measurements are different on this planet. Then, she takes me to Victoria's Inner Sanctum, where she waves the magic key card hanging around her neck and unlocks my dressing room. She fills out a card with my name and puts it in the slot outside the door, like they do with your file at the doctor's office. Then, she hands me two drawers with just about every bra style they make in my size, tells me to ring the button if I need her, and slam! The door shuts, sealing me in this tiny torture chamber with black walls, thirty bras, a fun house mirror, and some of the worst lighting I've ever seen in my life.

> *Slam! The door shuts, sealing me in this tiny torture chamber with black walls, thirty bras, a fun house mirror, and some of the worst lighting I've ever seen in my life.*

Then, I proceed to work up quite a dew, putting on and taking off bras. The culmination of this ordeal was buckling myself into one I couldn't get off. I kid you not! I mean, talk about attack of the Killer Bra! I'm thinking, to hell with the "service button," they need an emergency lever in here! That got me to giggling, which only got worse the more I yanked at the bra and tried to wiggle my way out of it. I would have made Houdini proud as I inched the thing over my hips thinking, I hope they don't have a secret camera recording this for YouTube!

I finally found a style that, through some miracle of modern engineering, managed to raise "the girls" up to where they should be, and give me a little cleavage to boot. Then, a different gal (I think) wrote the size and style on my card, and handed me over to another Brooke-Heather-Bri, who in turn took me back to the sales floor where she left me to paw through yet another drawer filled with a cornucopia of bras in my size and style: pink, red, turquoise, leopard print. Makes my head spin just thinking about it.

In the end, I bought two, one black and one flesh tone. So, with my coupon, I saved $10, spent $88, and got a free white cotton robe with Victoria's Secret emblazoned in big, gold letters on the back. Makes it all worthwhile, right?

Let this be a cautionary tale. Finding the right bra doesn't have to be hard. Since this ordeal, us girls have found a specialty place in Portland that's heaven. It's an intimate shop (feels more like a spa, really) where the saleswoman gives you two bras at a time to try on and really works with you to find the right fit. It's a little more expensive, but honey, it's worth every penny.

If you can't remember the last time you bought a new bra, it's time. Pamper yourself, and go to a place that specializes in really fitting you for a bra. The right bra will make your clothes look better and will trim about ten pounds off the way you look. Now that is a good secret!

Makeover Magic

Time for a makeover? You don't have to change the whole kit and kaboodle to spiff up your appearance and raise your spirits. Every little thing you do in this department helps you exercise your "I'm taking charge of my life" muscles. Start small. That way you won't get overwhelmed, and give up before you begin. Let's work from the top down.

To "Hair" is Human: Guys, this means you, too. If you're like Charlie, your wife told you when it was time for a hair cut. Or when to fire up the roto rooter and get to work on your nose hair. Now you're going to have to mark it on your calendar. Trust me, women notice these sorts of thing.

Gals, if you don't have a good hairdresser, find one. Ask your friends. If you see someone with a good cut or color, compliment them and ask for the name of their stylist. If you've been going to the same gal for ages and are in a rut, mix it up. I know, you're more loyal to your hairdresser than to your gynecologist, but you just lost your spouse. You can plead temporary insanity and finally get outta that dysfunctional relationship.

Try a new haircut, something you've been wanting to do for ages. Nothing too radical to start. Work into it. Change the color a little. Try highlights, low lights, a purple streak. If you've been dyeing your own hair, go to a salon and get a professional cut and color. A good colorist can work wonders.

Maybe you've been dyeing your hair and want to embrace your gray. Your stylist can help you go gray gracefully with temporary color. You do not have to look like Pepe le Pew for a year while it grows out! Seriously! If you're already gray but you feel it's a little drab, you can spiff up your look by using a shampoo that takes the yellow outta that gray. Gray is nature's highlights, and with a good cut, it can be real stylish!

Skin Deep: Take a look at your moisturizer and how you're cleansing your face. If you're still using the same lightweight stuff that you wore in your twenties, it may be time to amp it up a notch. You don't have to invest a fortune at a department store, either. There are some great drugstore brands that don't have a lot of perfume in them. Add in an eye cream while you're at it and something with a little more weight for night time. Once winter comes, you have to amp it up even more because it's so dry. If you're going to be outside in frigid temperatures, smear some really thick moisturizing cream on your face to protect it. I'm talkin' something just shy of Vaseline. You'll be surprised at what a difference it makes. And when you're moisturizing your face, don't forget your neck and décolletage (a fancy word for chest), too. A good moisturizer, eye cream, and night cream can work wonders and will make your skin look younger and help you look more rested. Don't forget to moisturize your body, too. You'll need a body moisturizer for summer and a more intense one for winter. And you can't moisturize your hands enough.

Speaking of your skin, if you don't already have a good dermatologist, find one. Again, recommendations from friends or your primary care doctor are key. Have a full body check to make sure there's nothing to be concerned about. But if you have age spots on your face, you don't have to suffer. They can work with you to do something about it. I know! It's a miracle! And don't leave the house without wearing a good sunscreen or "shade in a bottle," as my sister Irene calls it. Both the dermatologist and the sunscreen advice applies to you guys, too.

Natural, but Nicer: Sometimes, just changing up your lipstick can make you feel better. Or you could go for the whole makeover. For some people, doing this at the makeup counter of a department store can be intimidating. It's so public. Some people might prefer a spa, which sometimes sells cosmetics and is more relaxed. Always bring a friend you trust, someone who'll tell you the truth. Usually, there isn't a charge for this, because they're hoping to sell you the whole kit and caboodle. Hang tough. Go with a budget and stick with it. Maybe you just buy the lipstick (if you love the shade). Or, if you're like me, I put my money into my foundation and under-eye concealer. Then I buy the rest of the stuff (the flash, I call it) at the drug store.

Makeup isn't just for your face, either. I don't like those self tanners because you may end up looking like an oompa loompa. And it does not fade gracefully. That said, my days of sitting out in the sun greased up with baby oil and iodine are behind me. I'm not wearing panty hose during the summer, and without a tan, my legs can be a little lackluster. Well, I found this leg makeup that really does the trick. It's easy to apply, water resistant, and washes off in the shower.

Clothes Encounters: Guys and gals, take a hard look at your wardrobe. Clean out the old stuff, the things you haven't worn in, well, you can't even remember. This is about letting go of the old and making room for the new. If it's frayed or stained, say sayonara. If something needs to be altered, mended, or is missing a button, either fix it or hasta la vista, baby. Too small or too big, wave bye-bye.

Now comes the fun part: shopping!

Guys, you may not be as enthusiastic as I am about browsing around the mall. Maybe you ask for new stuff for your birthday or Christmas, or see if a friend will help you out. This goes for you, too, ladies. Shopping with a friend or group of friends is more fun and easier because you'll have someone to get you different sizes and such when you're in the dressing room. Plus, they'll be there to offer a second opinion. Sometimes it's hard to see what really looks good. I'm talking about paying attention to not only style, but color. Some colors work on you and some don't. If you're unsure, ask your friend. I bet they nail it right off the bat. And remember, as we get older, jeweltones are our best buddies.

Proper proportion is key. If you're under 5'4", shop in the petite section, and find a good seamstress. It's worth the money because if something doesn't look right, you're just not going to wear it. I still miss Mrs. Cloutier, who died about ten years ago. But I asked around and found a great gal, Ingrid, over in Dover-Foxcroft. She's a wiz. Get your pants, dresses, and skirts hemmed to the right length, sleeves, too. Look at your tops. Are they hitting in the right place? I like mine to come to just below "the barrel," I call it. If it hits down around my hips, it makes the lower half of my body look freakishly short. I have the short thing covered, and don't need to dress in a way that highlights it.

And don't forget shoes. Polish them. Get them reheeled. If they're beyond repair, get rid of 'em. That includes your stinky sneakers, too. The ones without any tread left on them. Get a nice new pair of cross trainers. Find a comfortable shoe with a little style to it. (It can be done.) Maybe a fun summer sandal. Heck, get some colorful socks to wear with your Birkenstocks. It's time to jazz it up!

I know! There are lots of suggestions here, and it sounds like a bunch of work. But, not only will spiffing things up make you feel better, it'll give you a project to occupy your time and, most importantly, your mind. Don't get overwhelmed. Start with the easiest thing you can do that will make a difference. It don't matter if it's so small no one else notices. If it puts a bounce in your step, go for it. Once again, this is all about taking care of your personal happiness.

Love Mahoosuc Mills Style: A Different Flavor Whoopie Pie

There's this gal, Doris, in my book group. She lost her husband Mike a few years back, and just last fall, she started dipping her toe back into the dating pool. Boy, that can't have been easy. But now she's seeing a nice fella, Gerry, that she met at church. I saw her the other day down to the Busy Bee.

"The weird thing is, Ida, Gerry couldn't be more different than Mike. Not just looks-wise, but in what he likes to do. You know, Mike was a big outdoors guy."

"Sure. Charlie always said he was a hell of a fisherman."

"He loved it. But Gerry's idea of camping? The Marriott."

"Now we're talking!"

"I know, right? He likes going to movies, out to eat. Treats me nice. Not that Mike didn't. He just wasn't much of a talker is all. And he was what you might call frugal."

"Sounds like you have a nice thing going with Gerry."

"You know, I do! And to think I turned him down for breakfast that first time. It was after church, and there were a few of us chatting in the parking lot. Gerry walked me to my car and asked if I wanted to get a bite to eat. I kind of panicked. 'Sorry,' I said, 'I have other plans.' I didn't, of course. The only thing I had planned was to go home and do laundry.

"But Gerry just smiles and says, 'Well, how about next week?' What could I say? I think I was kind of put off at first, because, you know, Mike was tall and rangy, with that nice head of hair and all."

"I do. He kind of had that Clint Eastwood thing going."

"And Gerry's kind of short and balding. He's not fat, exactly, but he has some meat on him. And that first date, well, it started off a little awkward. I was nervous as all get out. He was, too."

"I don't blame you."

"But I had my book with me for book group and he asked me about it, which in and of itself was startling, because Mike just never expressed interest in that kind of thing."

"Listen, Charlie doesn't exactly grill me about what I'm reading."

"Well, I told him the story as far as I'd gotten, and I'll be darned, he looked interested! Then he told me about the book he was reading. And I think that kind of relaxed us both. Our food came and we kept talking, like you do with a new friend. Just basic stuff, but it felt comfortable, you know? Then he asked me to go to Bangor the next week for dinner and a movie, and I said yes."

"I'm so happy for you, Doris."

"I'm happy, too. And trust me, Ida, I didn't think I was ever going to say that again. I still miss Mike, of course, but the good thing is, me and Gerry can talk about him. And Gerry's wife, too, because he's a widower. And it feels fine. It's nice to have someone to do things with, right? And we laugh a lot."

"Absolutely, Doris. Good for you! Oh look, Babe just put out some fresh whoopie pies. You want one? My treat."

"Hard to turn down one of Babe's famous whoopie pies."

"What kind do you want? I'm partial to the traditional chocolate."

"Funny thing, that used to be my favorite, too, but Gerry's got me hooked on the gingerbread whoopie pie with the maple cream frosting. Oh mister man, they're yummy!"

You're the New Star of The Bachelor(ette)

If you're ready to start dating again, remember, you are in the driver's seat. We've come a long way from Junior High with its giggling and "I wonder if he'll call" angst. Thank God!

The most important thing to remember is be clear about what you're looking for and what's a deal breaker. Basically, you've given up the illusion that you can change anyone and you're looking for a person who's done the same.

There are different approaches to meeting someone. You can be passive and keep doing what you're doing and hope lightening strikes. I'd put Doris in this category. You can be a joiner, join some senior groups, sign up for a class like ballroom dancing or take up a hobby that's done in a group, like bowling. Be friendly, but not aggressive. Focus on the task at hand, because it's fun and you may end up with a fringe benefit. If not, well, you've expanded your social circle and are having a good time.

Lastly, you can approach dating like a full-time job. You do everything the joiner's doing, but are a little more forthcoming. You ask your friends if they know anyone who might be a good match for you. And give computer dating a try while you're at it. It's a numbers game—the more you put yourself out there, the better the odds of meeting that special someone.

Computer Dating

My Dad tried the computer dating thing in a half-hearted way a few years back. He joined a Catholic dating site. A friend who's good with computers helped him put up his profile, but he didn't include a picture. When my niece Caitlin found out, she got Dad's password and added a nice photo of him taken at Easter dinner that year. I'll be darned. He got so many responses, it crashed his computer. Well, like I said, he's a good looking guy with nice head of hair and he still drives at night.

God, he's a character!

"How's the computer dating going, Dad?" I ask.

"I've been out on a few of dates."

"You have? Where'd you go?"

"We met at McDonalds for breakfast."

"Last of the big spenders."

"Hey, I was going anyway. I figured, why not have some company."

"How'd it go?"

"Alright, I guess, but it's hard to keep the women straight."

"Geez, how many dates you been on?"

"Three. See, they're all Catholic, about my age, so they were all named Mary. It's confusing."

"I can see that it would be."

"I ended up quitting the computer dating site because I was getting so many emails. Too much like work."

"Were any of the gals cute?"

"Nope. Women my age group fall into two categories: decent looking or I hope she's a good cook. All three definitely belonged in the second group."

Computer dating might not be for everyone, but you hear stories all the time about folks who met that way, fell in love, and lived happily ever after. If you're thinking about trying it, ask around and see if you know anyone who's given it a go. See if they have any tips. Why reinvent the wheel, right? Run your profile past a few friends to make sure it's working. And get clear about how much time you're going to devote to it.

I got a good tip from my friend Judy recently. She said if you're thinking about computer dating, search the internet for tips on how to be a good interviewer. Yes, the articles are all about the workplace, but they can be real helpful in a dating situation, too. Judy also recommends coffee dates. They're low impact, during the day, in a public place, and you can claim you have other commitments if it's not working. She's even taken to setting her phone alarm for forty-five minutes. It sounds like her ring tone, and, if she wants to end the date, Judy fakes an important conversation. This technique has gotten her outta a couple of "I'm so bored I'm gonna start tearing my hair out" debacles. If you're having a good time, you can tell him what you did, and laugh about it. If he doesn't laugh, well, that's a red flag.

Straight Talk From the Barcalounger: Heavy Packer

I'm relieved I'm not dating at this stage in the game. I know a few fellas down to work who are in the thick of it, and it's not for the faint of heart.

The older you get, the more baggage you come with. But some folks are lighter packers than others, if you know what I'm saying. And a few, well, they have a trailer load of baggage, and will start unpacking it at the drop of a hat. Expect you to help them sort though it. That can be tough going.

Word to the wise, if she needs a U-Haul for all her baggage and you're more of a carry-on kind of guy, move on.

Recipes for Romance: Newly Dating Dates

So you've had your coffee date, and you're interested. Maybe you're feeling a little spark or you just like how comfortable things are between you. It's time to really start dating.

Be creative. You're both on your best behavior, so now's the time to have fun and try different stuff. Because you know how it is once you get further into the relationship. The effort you're willing to put into it starts to wane. Trust me, there are things I used to do with Charlie in the early years that I'm just not willing to do anymore. Like big snowmobile trips—mile after mile, day after day of snowmobiling, like we're on a polar expedition, to get to some place, Presque Isle, for example. Which, don't get me wrong, is a nice little town, but (news flash) you can get there in less than half the time by driving and it's warmer! I did pick up some sturdy spouse points (as Dot calls 'em) for that particular excursion. I cashed those in later that year for a few days in Quebec City. We even stayed in a B&B that served tea at four. Still cracks me when I think of Charlie drinking tea and eating little cucumber sandwiches.

Anyhoo, now's the time to expand your horizons. Trust me, the bean suppers will still be there when you're ready to settle down. With the computer, it's a snap to find different kinds of things to do. Google festivals in your region. The Moxie Festival in Lisbon, Maine is a fave. Go on a whale watch or to an outdoor band concert. Try looking up "wacky things to do in New England" or whereever you live. Discover things like the Desert of Maine or America's Stonehenge. You get the idea. There was a great article in the *Bangor Daily News* a while back featuring eleven easy mountain hikes in Maine. How about diners or flea markets? Or both in one day? The world is full of possibilities. Now's the time to go out there and explore. And FYI, these kinds of things are fun with your friends, too, or your spouse, if they're still alive and kicking.

Living in Sin

Celeste's sister, Fran, lost her husband, Bob, seven years ago. It was sudden, a heart attack. And surprising, too, as Bob was in great shape, a runner. It's tough not to be able to say good-bye. One minute he's there, and the next, he's not.

As you can imagine, Fran had a hard time of it. Took her a good year to start sorting through his stuff. Didn't leave the house much. Just went to work and back, maybe stopped to buy a few groceries.

But she got the help she needed. She went on anti-depressants and joined a grieving group. Gradually, the cloud started to lift. Fran joined a walking group, and last year, she started taking ballroom dance lessons. Turns out she's pretty good at it. And that's where she met Phil.

The other day when us girls got together, I asked Celeste how they were doing.

"They moved in together," Celeste says.

"No!"

"Yes! Living in sin and loving it, Fran tells me."

"What did her kids think of that?"

"It took some adjusting. But she told 'em, 'I loved your father very much. Still do. Nothing can change that. I pray to him every day to not let me do anything stupid. But truth is I was so sad for so long, and Phil makes me happy. All I've ever wanted is for you kids is to be happy, and I hope that's what you want for me, too.'"

"Clever gal."

"Runs in the family," Celeste says with a wink. "Besides, Frannie and Phil are being smart about things. He's moved into her house, but is keeping his condo for now. Seeing how it goes. Eventually, they might sell their places and buy one together, but they're not ready just yet. They haven't blended any of their finances, either, which I think is smart."

"Good to keep your options open."

"That it is. Oh, Ida, when I see Frannie and Phil together, it does my heart good."

"I know how worried about her you were when Bob first died."

"Kept me up at night, thinking she might decide to follow him. Now, she looks so happy. Plus, I think she's had more sex in the last few months than Bud and I have had in a year."

"Gee, kind of makes me want to live in sin, too."

To Marry or Not to Marry

So, you've been dating awhile and have fallen in love again. Now what? To marry, or not to marry? That is the question. There is no right or wrong answer.

There are many options, but here are a few: You can follow Fran's lead and wade in slowly. See if you're compatible while living in the same house day after day. Or you may want to just dip your toe in. You can do that by traveling together. Go away for a weekend, then maybe a week. If you're retired and head south during the winter, rent a place with your sweetie for a month or two. This might be the perfect compromise. You live together some of the year, but still come home to the comfort and freedom of your own home.

Heck, you might not want to live together at all. There's nothing wrong with having a steady companion with an occasional sleepover.

Of course, you just might not feel comfortable living in sin. I get that. But before you decide to get married, weigh the pros and cons. Especially if you've already spent years nursing a sick spouse. Because let me tell you, in sickness and in health has a different meaning when you're in your twenties than in your sixties, seventies, or eighties.

If you're thinking of getting married, do some research. Go to your financial folks and see what the advantages and disadvantages are in terms of your money. Make sure you protect your kids in this department, and your new spouse, for that matter. That means if you haven't done a will and gotten your paperwork in order, do it now. I can't stress this enough because this kind of thing can go wrong in so many ways.

Say you're thinking about your new spouse selling their house and moving into your house, but you want to leave the house to your kids. Make sure your new spouse doesn't have to move out the minute you're gone. Maybe they have a certain amount of time to find a new home or they can stay there until they die. Conversely, leaving everything to your new spouse and depending on them to do right by your kids in a no-win situation. In the end, everyone is gonna be unhappy. Take your head outta the sand, make those hard decisions, and have those difficult conversations. Trust me, everyone concerned will appreciate your thoughtfulness long after you're gone.

Once you've thought it through, dotted your I's and crossed your T's, all the hard work's done. Now you can grab onto your second chance, hold 'em tight, and enjoy every minute of your time together.

Getting Goin'

- Time to let go of the hold button? Spiffing yourself up will help you get back into the flow of life. Start with your underwear drawer. Throw away anything that doesn't pass muster, then go buy new stuff.
- Get fitted for a new bra at a specialty bra shop. It will change your life!
- Look over the makeover section of this chapter, and pick one thing to try. Start with the easiest thing you can do that will make a difference in how you feel. Do it. If it doesn't kill you (and I'm pretty sure it won't), try another thing the next week. Maybe you choose to do one a week or one a month. And don't forget to ask your friends for help.

- Are you ready to start dating? Decide what you're looking for. What are your deal breakers? One person is not going to have every single thing you're looking for, but does three outta five work for you? Five outta seven?
- Want to try computer dating? Find someone you know who already has. Have a friend help you with your computer dating profile. Choose a photo where you look good, but is not 25 years old.
- Make a list of five fun dates. If you're not dating anyone, do them with a friend or by yourself.
- Have you found someone and are ready for the next step? Decide what you want, and think through your finances. Do what needs to be done, then get back to having fun together.

Epilogue

Charlie and me spent the weekend up to Dot and Tommy's camp recently with Dot and Tommy, of course, and Shirley and Junior. One of Charlie's favorite things about Dot and Tommy's camp is he gets to visit his old Barcalounger. Dot bought it at our yard sale. I'd been trying to get rid of the thing for years because it had seen better days (which is an understatement), but Charlie loved that old thing. The only way I could get him to let it go was to promise him it would go to a good home. The thing is, even though I'd gotten my way, I felt kind of bad for Charlie. Thank goodness Dot came to the rescue!

Oh, is he ever glad to see it! We arrive, Tommy hands him a Bud, and Charlie beelines it for his old recliner. He settles in to that mangy upholstery like it's some long, lost pal, and nothing short of fishing or the dinner bell will get him up again.

So, what did we do up to camp? Nothing that breaks a sweat, I'll tell you! Oh, the boys did some fishing: catch and release. Us girls love that because it gets them out of our hair. Plus, we don't have to clean and fry up the fish. It's a win/win.

The gals did a little cooking, of course, but mostly we just sat around and talked. There's a killer view of the lake from the screened-in porch. Better than TV! Dot and I love to rock on the squeaky old glider love seat. We rock at the same speed, which is probably a little faster than some people would like. Shirley goes, "You two think that glider's some kind of amusement park ride. I'm not sitting in that thing with either of you. It makes me sea sick!"

The camp is just plumb chucka full of old furniture and tacky knick-knacks that have somehow accumulated over the years. Dot bought the camp from her parents when it got too much for them. She hasn't changed it a lot because her folks still get up to camp a couple times a month during the summer. She wants them to still feel at home.

Every time we go up there, I discover some new treasure. I'm sitting at the table Saturday noon, when I see something brown and lumpy on top of the fridge.

"Dottie," I says. "What the hell is that?"

She takes the thing down from it's perch. "What does it look like?"

I study it hard. "I don't know. A big ceramic baked potato?"

"Got it in one!"

"That's one of the ugliest things I've ever seen." Shirley chimes in.

"Wait!" Dot goes. "There's a matching one in the cabinet, only bigger!"

"Serving bowls, right?" I ask, lifting the lid.

"Yup. But I've never had the stomach to use them."

Shirley goes, "So why don't you just get rid of 'em?"

"Believe me, the minute my mother goes, they go. I've tried to break it by accidentally dropping it on the floor, but it's not only ugly, it's indestructible."

I always get a kick out of these two ceramic animals hanging on the wall in the stairway up to the second floor. They kind of look like squirrels, but have buck teeth, so they could be beavers. It's hard to tell. We call them squeavers.

Dot has a nephew, Connor. He fancies himself a singer-songwriter (when he's not working down to The Home Depot), and last time he was at camp he come up with a limerick about them.

Have you heard of the North Country Squeaver?
He looks like an underachiever
His tail kind of curls
Like that of a squirrel
And his buck teeth are big as a beaver!

"Connor shouldn't quit his day job," Tommy joked.

They have an old stereo at camp and a killer assortment of vintage vinyl as my niece Caitlin would say. In the evening, we always play a few: Nat King Cole, Brenda Lee, and Elvis, of course. He's been gone over thirty years, but I still miss the King. When "All Shook Up" comes on, I catch Charlie's eye. That was the first song we danced to as husband and wife. A lot of water has passed under the bridge since then, but I remember it like it was yesterday. Charlie was so handsome in his white tux. I recall the look on his face as I walked down the aisle, my heart pounding, hardly feeling my feet on the floor. I was so happy. And you know what? Charlie can still make my heart go pitter-patter.

My favorite thing about camp, I think, is falling asleep to the loons. It's a lonesome sound, but comforting, too; a far away melody behind the rumble of my hubby's snoring.

Charlie and me got up at the crack of dawn, crept downstairs, out the door and went off for an early morning canoe ride. The lake was smooth as glass, mist floating over the water. Peaceful. Just the sounds of our paddling, insects buzzing and birds chirping, and that green smell of summer in Maine. We didn't really talk much. Didn't need to. It was just Charlie and me, enjoying each other's company.

We can smell the coffee brewing and bacon sizzling as we walk up from the dock, hand in hand. And yes, our friends tease us about sleeping in the canoe, again. We eat breakfast on the screened-in porch, overlooking the lake, all of us talking and laughing. Charlie smiles and squeezes my hand, looking so relaxed. And I think, at this moment, at this place here on Moose Megantic Lake, regardless of what we have been through, everything is wonderful in our world.

That's it for now. Catch you on the flip side!

Straight Talk From the Barcalounger: The Right Stuff

You can't change someone, and even if you could, that sounds like a lot of work to me. So, I guess if I had to sum up my take on how to have a happy marriage, I'd say make sure you marry the right gal. I did, and I thank my lucky stars every day.

Top three questions to ask yourself: Does she want the same things outta life? Is she easy to talk to? Does she get your jokes and vice versa? If you start out on the same page you have a good foundation for your marriage. Being able to talk to each other will help keep you on the same page because things change and so do you. You gotta be able to check in with each other, talk about stuff. And laughing together will make the good times even better and the hard times bearable. Everything else is gravy.

With the right gal, marriage might not always be easy, but it's definitely worth it.

Recipes for Romance: Whoopie Pie

I have to include a whoopie pie recipe here, right? I mean, how could I not? The thing is, I'm not the kind of gal who makes up recipes outta my head, but I'm very good at following directions. I mean, if a recipe told me to turn on the oven, dance a jig, then stand on my head, I'd do it.

I don't make whoopie pies that often. Why would I when I can get in my car, drive down to the Busy Bee and have one of Babe's beauties? But when I do, the recipe I use was printed in *Taste of Home* magazine some twenty years ago and is called Old-Fashioned Whoopie Pie. You can find it on the internet, I'm sure, along with oodles of other whoopie pie recipes.

As I said earlier, we're partial to the chocolate ones with a filling made of shortening and sugar, but I know some of you folks prefer yours with marshmallow fluff. Heck, you may not even want your traditional chocolate, and like something a little more exotic. Whatever floats your boat. You might have to experiment to see what's right for you.

Too much work? The internet is a wondrous thing. There are places that deliver homemade whoopie pies to your door. God bless America! I'm partial to Wicked Whoopie Pies based in Gardiner. Or make an adventure out of it. Go on a whoopie pie mission. Find the bakery that makes the best whoopie pies in your town, state or heck, in the country. Talk about a grand slam. You're combining a bucket list item (find the best whoopie pie) with destination eats, a road trip and quality time with your spouse!

Acknowledgments

Firstly, I'd like to thank all the fine folks at Islandport Press. Editor Genevieve Morgan originally expressed interest in the idea of this book and asked to see a proposal. Katy Kelleher contributed editing suggestions. Thank you to Jennifer Hazard, my blog editor. (A lot of the stories in this book began as blogs.) A big thank you goes to Theresa Lagrange for her wonderful book cover design and Michelle Lunt for the overall look of the book. And thank you to Shannon Butler and Holly Eddy for helping to get my books out of the warehouse and into the hands of readers, and Melissa Kim and Taylor McCafferty for all you do. A special thanks to Dean Lunt for editing and having such a great understanding of Ida and feel for the state of Maine.

Next, I'd like to thank the women in my writers group: Kathy Gunst, Marie Harris, Grace Mattern, and Mimi White for their ongoing support and encouragement. Thank you as well to my dear friend Liz Korabek-Emerson for her story about saving money which appears in Chapter 5's "Love Mahoosuc Mills: Getting Motivated." Nancy Euchner of AgeQuest was extremely helpful in walking me through many of the strategies that appear in Chapters 8 and 9. Thanks to Ann Carlton for sharing her bike story which serves as the foundation for "Just Like Riding a Bike" in Chapter 7, and to Janet Mitchko for her sage advice on computer dating. My great-aunt and uncle, Celina and Henry Chamberland, who serve as the inspiration for Ida and Charlie's friends of the same name, and our next door neighbors, Doug and Carmen Brunell, for Hank and Pearl Plaisted.

How can I not thank the great state of Maine and all the Maine-iacs who reside here? You inspire me every day. Dot and

Tommy's camp is central to the book, and is kind of a hybrid between the camp I remember as a kid owned by my uncle and aunt, Raymond and Germaine Poulin on Ripley Pond and the one owned by Aunt Celeste and Uncle David Nichols on Schoodic Lake. I have such fond memories of visiting Uncle Raymond and Aunt Germaine's camp as a kid. I especially remember how much fun all the adults were having: racing canoes, drinking barley juice for breakfast and laughing up a storm, as Ida would say. Celeste and David's camp is now owned by my cousin Maureen Nichols, and we try to visit when we can. It's a homey place with a glider on the screened in porch, old books on the shelves, squeavers adorning the walls and the sound of loons lulling us to sleep.

My husband Gordon and I live in an amazing community. Thank you to Kathy, John, Marie, and Charter for recently bringing that home to us. And to all our friends and fans for your support, thank you so much!

A big, heartfelt thanks goes to my mother and father, Betty and Pat Poulin, whose marriage and life philosophy inspires much of this book. And thanks and gratitude to my sister, Jane Poulin, for her constant friendship and support, and for inspiring Irene and all the good times she shares with Ida.

And Gordon, thank you for being my collaborator in art and in life. For sharing your talent so generously with me, for the icons that appear in this book, for your writing and editing feedback, and for making sure Ida continues to sound like Ida.

Thanks each and every one of you!

May, 2016

About Susan Poulin

If you've ever seen Ida LeClair on stage, or if you've ever turned to the witty, wise Mainer for advice, then you already know Susan Poulin. Actress, author, and former housecleaner, Poulin has been performing as Ida for years—ever since she debuted her one-woman show, *Ida: Woman Who Runs with the Moose* back in 1997.

On the surface, Poulin and LeClair couldn't be more different. Poulin studied theater at the University of Southern Maine. LeClair studies the shoppers who come through her checkout line at the A&P. Poulin owns a production company, Poolyle Productions and has performed on stages throughout New England and New York. LeClair owns a double-wide and has spent years perfecting her meatloaf and Whoopie Pie recipes. But they are both warm and giving, funny, and smart.

In her first book, *Finding Your Inner Moose*, Poulin (writing as LeClair) tells her readers how to live a happier life. Peppered with humorous anecdotes, both fictional and drawn from Poulin's experiences in Maine, the book served as a perfect companion to her nine live shows, including *Ida's Havin' a Yard Sale*, *A Very Ida Christmas*, and *I Married an Alien*. Her most recent book, *The Sweet Life*, builds upon the advice laid down in *Finding Your Inner Moose*, but with a slightly different focus. This time, Poulin tackles the ooey-gooey stuff of life: dating, marriage, and long-term love.

When Poulin isn't performing as Ida, or scheming up new books, she can be found online, updating her weekly humor blog, *Just Ask Ida*. She works from her home in Eliot, Maine, where she lives with her husband and collaborator, Gordon Carlisle, and her sweet dog Charlie.